An Ignatian Pathway

Experiencing *THE* Mystical Dimension *OF THE* Spiritual Exercises

PAUL COUTINHO, SJ

LOYOLA PRESS.
A JESUIT MINISTRY
Chicago

LOYOLAPRESS.
A JESUIT MINISTRY

3441 N. Ashland Avenue
Chicago, Illinois 60657
(800) 621-1008
www.loyolapress.com

Scripture texts are from the New Revised Standard Version Bible: Catholic Edition, copyright © 1993 by Catholic Bible Press. Reprinted by permission.

References to St. Ignatius' *Autobiography* are from *St. Ignatius' Own Story As Told to Luis Gonzalez de Camara,* translated by William J. Young, SJ. © 1998 Jesuit Way. Chicago: Loyola Press. All rights reserved.

References to the *Spiritual Exercises* are from *The Spiritual Exercises of St. Ignatius,* translated by Louis J. Puhl, SJ. © 1951 The Newman Press. Chicago: Loyola Press. All rights reserved.

References to the *Spiritual Journal* are from *The Spiritual Journal of St. Ignatius Loyola: February, 1544 to 1545,* translated by William J. Young, SJ. © 1958. Woodstock, MD: Woodstock College Press. All rights reserved.

Cover image: Sandra Prietz/iStockphoto/Thinkstock

Library of Congress Cataloging-in-Publication Data
Coutinho, Paul.
 An Ignatian pathway : experiencing the mystical dimension of The spiritual exercises of Saint Ignatius of Loyola / Paul Coutinho.
   p. cm.
 ISBN-13: 978-0-8294-3309-8
 ISBN-10: 0-8294-3309-0
 1. Ignatius, of Loyola, Saint, 1491-1556. Exercitia spiritualia. 2. Mysticism--Catholic Church. I. Title.
 BX2179.L8C666 2011
 248.3--dc22

                                                              2010053238

Printed in the United States of America
11 12 13 14 15 16 Bang 10 9 8 7 6 5 4 3 2 1

To you, dear reader,

who seek the deeper meaning and fullness of life.

Contents

Note to the Reader

The Spiritual Exercises of St. Ignatius were meant to be a pathway to the mystical life. The mystical gifts and graces that Ignatius received are not reserved for a select few, but are available to anyone who follows the Spiritual Exercises. In fact, according to Ignatius, the mystical life seems to be the culmination of any spiritual pathway.

This book is an attempt to get to the core of Ignatius's mystical heart. It translates good scholarship into a language and method that anyone can follow. This book is also an attempt to correct faulty English translations that have prevented people from becoming like Ignatius—mystics in everyday life.

If those who are giving the Ignatian Exercises and those making them are not exposed to the original dynamic that Ignatius intended, these sincere people will continue to invest time and money in the Ignatian tradition and not experience the real effect of the Ignatian pathway—namely, living the fullness of life in peace, joy, and inner freedom.

For anyone who wants to live the fullness of life, I hope that this book offers infinite possibilities. The Ignatian

Spiritual Exercises greatly benefit the scholar and the beginner. Likewise, this book can be used by individuals and by groups, by directors and by individuals who are looking to deepen their spiritual life, or by those looking to be mystics in everyday life. Groups of people who want to be trained in the Spiritual Exercises—trainers and trainees and those who are committed to spiritual direction—can all profit from using this book.

This book is the result of my forty-three years of studying and experiencing the Ignatian pathway both in my personal life and in teaching, directing, and training others in different parts of Asia, Europe, Africa, Oceania, and the United States. My understanding has been tested through workshops, seminars, and keynote talks at different national and international conferences. I am grateful for this opportunity to share with you my perspective and experience of Ignatius and the Spiritual Exercises.

Paul Coutinho, SJ
September 2010

Introduction

St. Ignatius has been characterized in many different and sometimes contradictory ways. His spirituality has been defined in military terms, and at the same time it is difficult to get away from the fact that he is a man who lives fully on the affective level. He is not afraid of expressing his emotions with tears or heavy sobbing. His language and vocabulary reflect the chivalry, courage, and romance of the knights of the Middle Ages. Ignatius has been accused of contrary heresies: quietism, which fosters total inaction and passivity in our relationship with God; and Pelagianism, where one reaches spiritual perfection by one's effort alone. For some, Ignatian spirituality belongs to the sixteenth-century Council of Trent where the Catholic Church defined itself against what it considered Protestant heresies, and so Ignatian spirituality is outdated. For others like Karl Rahner, a Jesuit and one of the most influential theologians of the twentieth century, Ignatius belongs to the future. And that future is now!

The spirituality that Ignatius lived and developed has become a spiritual methodology, and it is also more than a method—it is a way of life. Ignatius developed several methods of spiritual practice through the experience of his own life, and he recorded these in his *Autobiography* (AB), his *Spiritual Journal* (SpJ), and in his collection of *Spiritual Exercises* (SE). Ignatius testifies in his *Autobiography* that "the Exercises were not composed all at one time, but things that he had observed in his own soul and found useful and which he thought would be useful to others, he put into writing" (AB 99). The *Spiritual Exercises* were not written as an academic exhortation or as a result of academic studies. Rather, they are a result of God drawing Ignatius into intimacy with the Divine. For Ignatius, God was not confined to and defined by any one religion, whereas the Divine and the Infinite expressed the essence of this God. The Divine and the Infinite cannot be defined but experienced.

One of the primary methods of Ignatian spirituality is to be open to experience, to reflect on that experience, and to have the courage to renew our lives in the light of the discerned meaning of our experience. The Ignatian understanding of experience is to find our personal identity in the Divine and the interconnectedness of all of life. Our reflection is not on ourselves or what we have been doing, but rather it is a certain sensitivity to and an awareness of God working in us. It is God who is drawing us more and more into a divine union and communion. As a fruit of this reflection, we open ourselves more and more to *receive* God into the depths of our being and allow that divine presence, power, and essence to flow into our relationship with people, our work, and life itself.

Personal experience was paramount for Ignatius. His experience of the Divine became an absolute in his life and everything else was influenced by this experience. He speaks about this in no uncertain words in his *Autobiography*, which is a testament of his relationship with the Divine: "These things which he saw gave him at the time great strength, and were always a striking confirmation of his faith, so much so that he has often thought to himself that if there were no Scriptures to teach us these matters of faith, he was determined to die for them, merely because of what he has seen" (AB 29). Ignatius considers himself to be a pilgrim on a spiritual journey through life. He understands that his mystical journey is a journey of every human being, and therefore talks about himself in the third person.

Sometimes even the Church's teaching and practice were subject to Ignatius's spiritual experience. While writing the *Constitutions of the Society of Jesus*, which is a spiritual pathway for the Jesuits, Ignatius's first companions would often question him about some of the things that went contrary to the teaching of the Church on religious life. Ignatius would reply, "I saw it at Manresa," and rest his case. The companions had lived long enough with Ignatius to know that once he quoted Manresa he would not budge from his stand. Ignatius came to Manresa, the center of Catalonia, Spain, in 1522 and spent almost a year near the river Cardoner, which runs through the town. It was here that Ignatius stopped finding God, but allowed God to find him. It was here that he learned to receive all that God wanted to give him. At Manresa his life began to change so radically, and he received so many graces, that Ignatius compared his experience with St. Paul's experience on the road to Damascus. The Manresa experience became for Ignatius the criterion by which he would live the rest of his life. Ignatius believed that at Manresa he was taught directly by God, who "treated him just as a schoolmaster treats a little boy when he teaches him. . . . he thought that any doubt about it would be an offense against His Divine Majesty" (AB 27).

Ignatius was so convinced that God speaks directly with individuals that he strongly advises that those who direct the Spiritual Exercises ". . . should permit the Creator to deal directly with the creature, and the creature directly with his Creator and Lord" (SE 15). The role of the retreat directors is to help the retreatant to come into the presence of God, and then to disappear or move out of the way. They point to the Lamb of God like John the Baptist did—God must increase, and they decrease. They are like the matchmaker who does not go on the honeymoon.

Ignatius is comfortable with making our personal experience the criterion for all action because the more we allow ourselves to receive and deepen our relationship with the Divine, the more our soul "is inflamed with love of its Creator and Lord, and as a consequence, can love no creature on the face of the earth for its own sake, but only in the Creator of them all" (SE 316).

Ignatian Spiritual Landmarks

I would like us to journey together with the great pilgrim, Ignatius. Our one desire and choice on this journey should be what is more conducive to the end for which we are created namely, to praise, reverence, and serve God our Lord (SE 23). We live in intimacy with the Divine, are drawn into greater union and communion with the Divine Essence, and experience interconnectedness with all of life. This, I believe, is the cornerstone of the Ignatian pathway and the *Spiritual Exercises*.

As a hospital chaplain, I was once called to the bedside of a man who was afraid of dying. I saw his family around him and thought he was afraid to leave his family to fend for themselves. I would have understood his fear if he were afraid of dying because he had things to do and places to go, but that was not the case. This man was afraid of dying because he was afraid of meeting God. And the astounding thing was that this man had made forty-five retreats at a Jesuit retreat house. I often wondered what kind of a God was talked about that, after forty-five retreats, the man was afraid of meeting God!

When I share this experience with priests and religious, it is amazing to find how many of the senior men and women identify with this man. They are afraid of dying because they are afraid of meeting God. They are afraid because they hardly know God.

If the way we relate with God and our prayer has not changed in the last few years, then maybe, just maybe, we might not know God, nor have a relationship with God. Perhaps we have a theology, a concept, or some idea that has been passed down to us, often riddled with fear, anxiety, and guilt. The *Spiritual Exercises* of Ignatius will introduce us to a relationship with the living God and help us grow into mystics who live the fullness of life in peace and freedom.

What does it mean to have a relationship with God and see the face of the Divine? One way to understand this is to discover our fundamental grace. Each of us has one fundamental grace. Sometimes this grace is revealed through a foundational experience. It is important to recognize our foundational experience because all the other graces in our life will be a deepening or an expression of that one grace. That grace will give us the authority for the life that we live and the things that we do. In times of crisis, when everything seems dark and hopeless, we will fall back on the grace of our foundational experience to find our purification and enlightenment, to see what is real and what is not. Our foundational experience is often expressed as the meaning and the message of our lives and keeps us connected in continual relationship with God.

Ignatius gives us a method of discovering our fundamental grace. He invites us to go over our lives year by year, period by period, to become aware of our experiences at different places we have lived and reflect on our relationships with people and our work. We will see the pattern that sustained us and kept us alive and moving ahead in life. In that pattern we will discover our fundamental grace. Ignatius will show us how to name that grace and make it the focus of our life and the source of our inspiration and strength at all times.

Ignatius recognized his fundamental grace when he had his foundational experience at Manresa. He had found his absolute in God. During the battle of Pamplona, Ignatius was wounded by the French while he was defending a fortress for the honor of Spain. While he was convalescing in his home, the castle of Loyola, he reflected on the flow of his life, and he was deeply affected by reading the *Life of Christ* and the *Lives of the Saints*. He frequently read passages from these two books and experienced a deep affection for what he read. He spent a long time reflecting on the experience, soaking it in, and then letting the experience permeate every aspect of his life. In this process he was assimilated into the Trinity through Christ, and through the Trinity found himself in the Divine Essence. Ignatius's way of relating with God helped him live a life of continual consolation.

Ignatius had the habit of keeping a journal of his experiences. He also kept notes of things that helped him and which might help others later. When he set out as a pilgrim on a spiritual path, he carried these notes with him. He decided to spend a few days in Manresa to finish writing his experiences. The few days turned into eleven months, and the few notes into the *Spiritual Exercises*.

At Manresa the eyes of his understanding began to be opened, and the consciousness of the Divine transformed him. Ignatius expressed his foundational experience as the *magis*—the ever greater. The experience of the *magis* was the meaning, the message of his life, and gave his life power, authority, and efficacy. The *magis* is not measured by what Ignatius does, but by the ever-deepening relationship with the Divine. The *magis* then, is a divine relationship of infinite possibilities.

The Ignatian Graces Are Not a Privilege But a Right

Ignatius believed that all the graces he received are available to anyone following his pathway. St. Paul, in his letter to the Galatians, reminds us that we are sons and daughters of God and therefore heirs. And so the graces of God are not a privilege but our right. All those graces that Ignatius received are ours by the very nature of our pathway to God.

Let us examine some of the graces Ignatius received at Manresa (AB 28–30) that we need to make our very own. The first grace that Ignatius talks about is an insight into God, who is the Trinity. He sees the Trinity as a musical chord, three notes but one sound. This is an affective experience through the senses, and not a theology reflected by three musical notes on a music sheet. He noticed that, at this time, he made four prayers to the Trinity without understanding why. The significance of that fourth prayer will unfold as Ignatius pursues his spiritual quest.

Ignatius's spiritual journey brings him to La Storta. Ignatius always looked for companions with whom he could share his rich spiritual experiences. He had gathered a group of men, like Francis Xavier and Peter Faber. After they were ordained priests, they decided to offer themselves to be at the disposal of the pope. After he was ordained, Ignatius spent a year in preparation for the celebration of his first Mass. During this time he also prayed constantly to Mary to deign to place him with her Son. Ignatius wanted to be one of Jesus' knights and be part of establishing the kingdom of God here on earth. On their way to Rome, Ignatius stopped at a little chapel in La Storta, just outside the city of Rome. While Ignatius went in to pray, the gifts and graces of Manresa came alive, and his relationship with the Divine deepened as he saw in a vision how Mary had answered his prayer.

In this little chapel, Ignatius had a vision where he saw God the Father asking Jesus, who was carrying his cross, to take Ignatius as his companion. Jesus then turned to Ignatius and accepted him to serve them. This experience was very Pauline. Like Paul, Ignatius is conformed to the Son. Like Paul, he has the consciousness of the Son. Like Paul, he has become one with the Son and can exclaim, "It is no longer I who live, but it is Christ who lives in me" (Galatians 2:20).

Each time that Ignatius believes he has reached the ultimate or peak experience, something even more wonderful occurs. It happens because he is open to receive the experience and because he believes in a spirituality of infinite possibilities. God, who is limitless, continues to do great things for him and draws him into a deeper relationship with the Divine.

On February 27, 1544, Ignatius makes this very profound entry in his *Spiritual Journal*, ". . . and going into the chapel and praying, I felt or rather saw beyond my natural strength the Most Holy Trinity and Jesus, presenting me, or placing me, or simply being the means of union in the midst of the Most Holy Trinity" (SpJ, I–26). Following this spirituality of infinite possibilities, Ignatius, who was placed with the Son at La Storta, now becomes one with the Most Holy Trinity.

Can Ignatius's relationship with the Divine go deeper than the Trinity? Yes. On March 6, in that same journal, Ignatius shares his experience of being lost in the very being and essence of God: "I felt and saw, not obscurely, but clearly and very clearly, the very Being or Essence of God, under the figure of a sphere, slightly larger than the appearance of the sun" (SpJ, I–34). The "felt and saw" of Ignatius is an experience of the deepest or highest contemplation. Ignatius "felt and saw" not with his head, nor in his heart, but through pure consciousness. On March 6, 1544, being lost in the very being and essence of the Divine became an expressed reality for Ignatius. Ignatius died in 1556. One begins to wonder where these infinite possibilities finally took him in his relationship with the Divine.

The second grace that Ignatius received at Manresa is his experience of creation. He saw the whole of creation coming from God, going back to God, and the whole of creation in God. Ignatius's response to this experience of creation is one of reverence. This reverence is an expression of spiritual repose and a sign of being contemplative in action.

Reverence, that is, *acatamiento*, which is a self-emptying process in order to be filled with the Divine, becomes *the* Ignatian attitude. This *acatamiento* can be expressed as devotion, which is a means of total commingling with the divine presence. If we read his *Spiritual Journal*, whenever Ignatius talks about *acatamiento*, or reverence, he loses his power of speech, his hair stands on end, and he has chemical changes in his body. Ignatian reverence, then, is a physical experience in this union and communion with the Divine.

On March 14, 1544, Ignatius will write in the *Spiritual Journal* that God was giving him a gift that was of more value than all his other gifts. That was the gift of reverence. "When the tears came I repressed them . . . I was persuaded that a higher value was placed on this grace (*acatamiento*) and knowledge for the spiritual advantage of my soul, than on all those that went before (SpJ, II–2)." This is Ignatius's experience of creation, which is reflected in the *Spiritual Exercises* and becomes a very effective means of deepening his union and communion with the Divine Essence. If there is one attitude that distinguishes a follower of Ignatius, it should be *acatamiento*, or reverence.

This was followed by the experience of how Jesus is present in the Eucharist (AB 29). From then on the Eucharist becomes the center of Ignatius's spirituality, his spiritual life, and his prayer. It was also the occasion of his many visions and mystical graces. In fact, when Ignatius writes to Francis Borgia, the Duke of Gandia who later became the Superior General of the Jesuits, he tells him that the Eucharist is the surest and most direct way to union and communion with the Divine. The Eucharist will become an effective means for us on the Ignatian pathway.

Next, Ignatius talks about his insight into the humanity of Jesus. Ignatius sees the humanity of Jesus without distinguishing members of his body. For Ignatius, Jesus is neither masculine nor male. Jesus is a divine person—and in the humanity of Jesus, Ignatius experiences the whole being of God. He experiences Mary in the same way. And so, in the humanity of Jesus, Ignatius experienced what he experienced in creation and the Eucharist—the very being or essence of the Divine. As we go through the mysteries of Christ in the Spiritual Exercises, we need to make sure that we contemplate Christ as Emmanuel, God-with-us.

Ignatius thus found his fundamental grace, the core of his being, at Manresa. All the graces that preceded Ignatius's foundational experience are available in the Spiritual Exercises to help us to find our fundamental grace.

The *Spiritual Exercises:* The Ignatian Pathway

Ignatius always reflected on his life and experiences, and those things that he found useful he put down in writing so that others might also profit from his personal gifts and methods. This method is spelled out in the *Spiritual Exercises.* These Exercises are the surest and most direct gateway to all the graces that Ignatius received. We develop an intimacy with the Divine and experience the interconnectedness of all of life.

The *Spiritual Exercises* begins with a section that clarifies the goal of all that is to follow, the strengths and the obstacles that we will encounter on this spiritual adventure (SE 1–22). This section culminates in the Ignatian "Principle and

Foundation" (SE 23) of all his spirituality. He states the goal of our lives, the role of creatures, and our attitude of indifference that will ultimately help us make the "Contemplation to Attain the Love of God" our way of life (SE 230–237).

Ignatius divides the *Spiritual Exercises* into four weeks, but these are not literally four weeks of seven, twenty-four-hour days. These are four progressive stages that take us deeper and deeper into an intimacy with God, the Divine Essence. The First Week focuses on our relationship with God. It climaxes in "a cry of wonder with surging emotions" (SE 60) when we experience God's total and unconditional love for us personally. In the Second Week we continue to deepen this experience and our relationship with God by contemplating the hidden and public life of Jesus, Emmanuel, God-with-us. In the Third Week, as we contemplate the passion and death of our Lord, we identify with the heart and spirit of the suffering Jesus. In the Fourth Week we find ourselves totally lost and found in the Divine. We experience this same essence in every creature.

These Exercises can be made either in thirty consecutive days in a secluded place and in complete silence (SE 20), or they can be adapted to a weekend or an eight-day retreat (SE 18). There is also a third way to experience the graces of the Ignatian pathway. We can stay at home in the midst of our daily lives, spending many months tasting and savoring the gifts of God's life and love as we go through the dynamic of the Spiritual Exercises (SE 19). This book is intended to help readers make the Spiritual Exercises in this third way.

Prayer in the *Spiritual Exercises*

Prayer for Ignatius is not an end in itself, but a means to deepen our relationship with the Divine and experience the many graces that Ignatius himself experienced. Ignatian prayer can be divided into three major levels: meditation, which is the prayer of the mind; contemplation, the prayer of the heart; and the "Application of the Senses," which is the prayer of consciousness. In meditation, one receives revelations and ends by making resolutions. In contemplation, one opens oneself to the mystery and allows the mystery to fill and transform the one praying. The "Application of the Senses" is the prayer where neither the head nor the heart comes in the way of pure consciousness. It is through the Ignatian prayer of consciousness that one is on the road to making contemplation a way of life.

The Method, or Way of Proceeding

It is very important to be familiar with the text of the *Spiritual Exercises*, and it is necessary to find a good English translation (the one by Louis J. Puhl, SJ is preferred). Remember that the numbers referred to in the text are not page numbers but divisions within the *Spiritual Exercises*.

We need to set aside about an hour each day to take in all the gifts and graces that are available to us in the Spiritual Exercises. We begin by spending ten to fifteen minutes in preparation for prayer. Then we read the matter for the day from this book. We pray for an ever-deepening experience of the Divine in our relationship with God, and for the grace to empty ourselves of all distractions. We make ourselves available to God so that God can work wonders in us.

We find a prayerful place, either in our own homes, or in a church, or even in some peaceful place in nature. It might be helpful to use the same place every day and create our sacred space. We take a comfortable, prayerful posture and begin by focusing on the air we breathe. When we breathe in, we imagine breathing in the divine energy and presence. When we breathe out, we let go of our tension, anxieties, and all negative energy. We can do this breathing exercise for about five minutes, or until we find our hearts and minds composed and ready for divine presence.

We spend about a half hour praying over the mystery or the theme for the day. Remember the aim of our prayer is not to find God but to allow God to find us. We open our minds and hearts to the mystery we are contemplating. We listen with our hearts and allow ourselves to be confirmed in the things we already know, to clarify those things that we are curious about or struggle with, and to be challenged to go beyond sacred boundaries seeking new horizons. We let our prayer experience and insights seep into our innermost being and crystallize into a way of being.

After our prayer, we spend another ten or fifteen minutes reflecting on how God was affecting our lives in our prayer. We keep a journal of this prayer experience. Our prayer experience becomes the background of our day and permeates everything that happens to us. At the end of the day we are grateful for this experience and pray for a deepening of this grace.

At the end of every Ignatian week, or stage, we write out a summary of all our experiences. We might want to make this summary material our prayer, to savor and relish the presence and love of God until we are sufficiently satisfied.

It will be very helpful to find a spiritual director. This person does not have to be a priest or a religious, but one who has a deep relationship with God. It will be good to talk to this director either once a week or when we are ready to share the fruits we have gathered

Once we have gone through the whole dynamic of the Spiritual Exercises as spelled out in this book, we can use our prayer journals to deepen our experiences. At least once a month read through the overall summary of the experience of the entire Spiritual Exercises. On weekend or annual retreats, take the summaries of every week of the Spiritual Exercises and deepen the prayer experience. We pray over those parts of the book where we found consolation, when we were drawn toward God, or desolation, when we were drawn away from God.

We follow this method from one stage to the next, ever deepening our love and our relationship with the Divine. Like Ignatius, we will find our identity in the Divine and experience the interconnectedness of all of life.

Days of Preparation

The Goal of Life

For Ignatius the finality of all of life is in the Divine Essence. The preparatory prayer that Ignatius suggests we pray before all that we do reflects this "Principle and Foundation" (SE 46). We pray that all our intentions, actions, and operations may be directed wholly to the praise and service of the Divine Majesty.

Our intentions are formed by an awareness of our deep inner longings. Our hearts were made for God and they will be restless until they rest in God. This is what St. Augustine believed, and this is also reflected in Ignatius. The preparatory prayer is a way for us to harness this inner drive and channel it into every moment of our lives.

We are made to experience intimacy with the Divine.

✠ 2

The Whole of Creation

The whole of creation comes from God, goes back to God, and is in God. Creation finds its identity in God and the interconnectedness of all of life. This is the principle and the foundation of Ignatian spirituality. Ignatius believed that those who grow in the spiritual life will constantly contemplate how the Divine is present in every creature. (SE 39)

The Bible begins by introducing us to the Divine breath that hovered over the chaos and darkness. This breath was then poured into all of creation. God breathed this breath into humans and we became alive. We are made in the Divine image and likeness. The Divine breath gives us our identity and connects us with the rest of creation. All will pass away, but the Divine breath will remain forever.

The Divine breath of God is the very air we breathe.

The Journey, Not the Destination

Ignatius tells me that I am a pilgrim on a spiritual journey. I come to see that the orientation or the disposition of my life is more important than the final outcome I seek. The patterns of our lives are more important than the details of our personal history. The process of discernment is more important than the decisions I reach.

That's why Ignatius is more interested in the *why of things than the what*. He wants to know why we sin rather than the list of our sins. Ignatius wants us to spend our energy living our lives well rather than straining to figure out why we are in the situations we find ourselves in.

Ignatius called himself a pilgrim. I am a pilgrim. You are a pilgrim. And so with Ignatius we need to put on the mind of the pilgrim and set forth on a journey.

The moment the pilgrim decides to settle down, the pilgrim dies.

✛ 4

Dancing with Your Shadow

Ignatius believes that every person has just one root sin and all the other sins are an expression of that one sin. Similarly, we have just one grace and all the other graces are a deepening of that one grace. What is amazing is that the root sin and the root grace share the same energy. When we come to this realization we will be able to use the energy of our root sin to deepen and bring to life our root grace.

In the life of Ignatius we find that his root sin, or his shadow, is vainglory. He begins the testimony of his life by stating that during the first twenty-six years of his life he was a man given to the vanities of the world (AB 1). This shadow stayed with him until the end of his life. But Ignatius made vainglory work for him when the ever-greater glory of God—*ad maiorem dei gloriam* (AMDG)—became his principle and driving force for doing everything. This AMDG later became the motto of the Society of Jesus, which he founded.

Ignatius offers us the method that worked in his own life (SE 56). He wants us to find our way of proceeding in our sinful life (*el proceso de los pecados*). He suggests that we determine the dynamics of our root sin by going over our life year by year and from period to period, looking at our experiences with the people, places, and work that we were involved in. This dance and romance with our shadow brings us to our root grace with an exclamation of wonder (SE 60) and climaxes in a life of growing inner freedom as we move toward total immersion in God (SE 237).

Power is made perfect in weakness.

✠ 5

Getting Rid of Our Baggage

Pilgrims travel light. The travel kit becomes simpler as it is emptied, little by little—material things, theological doctrines, spiritual experiences, and even our present relationship with God. As these clouds go away we get a glimpse of what is beyond—the sun, the moon, the stars, and the myriad galaxies. Jesus refers to the kingdom of God as a person who is looking for a fine pearl or a treasure hidden in a field, and when these are found, one is ready to sell everything for that pearl or treasure (Matthew 13:44–46).

The pilgrim is totally focused on the pearl and the treasure: deepening the relationship with the person of the Divine and the Infinite. The pilgrim keeps moving, not only physically but also intellectually, emotionally, and spiritually.

Just as a river keeps fresh by flowing, a holy person keeps holy by steadily moving along the path.

Thoughts, Feelings, Prayers

The beginning and the end of the day affect our spiritual and psychological life in a very significant way. Ignatius warns us to be very careful about the thoughts and feelings that we have while we fall asleep (SE 73). These thoughts and feelings that we entertain will sink deep into our subconscious and unconscious selves and affect our waking lives in a significant way.

Before we go to sleep, Ignatius wants us to sum up the prayer that we will make when we awake. We think about the grace that we expect to experience in our prayer. Like our last thoughts at night, our first thoughts in the morning are also important. And when these two moments are connected, the time in between is very influenced by these thoughts and go deep into our subconscious and the unconscious. In fact, our first conscious moment of the day will often decide how the rest of the day will flow.

Ever since I was a kid I have always gone to bed thanking God for the gifts and the blessings of the day, and I begin my day with the sign of the cross. Before any other thoughts and feelings, the sign of the cross sets the stage for my day. This prayer is now an automatic action; I do not even have to think about the words that go with it. The day begins with God, and will flow with God, and come to a spiritual end of a wonderful day.

Our thoughts and feelings are intertwined.

Preparing for Prayer

Ignatius takes great care over the setting of his prayer. For Ignatius, prayer isn't something you just do. You approach it carefully. Ignatius does not want us to rush into prayer. Our preparation for prayer is as important as the prayer itself. Ignatius wants us to empty ourselves of all selfishness so that we are able to receive all that God wants to give us. Ignatius suggests that we make an act of humility and reverence as a physical sign of our inner self-emptying and our preparation to receive God into our innermost selves.

Just before we begin our prayer, we look at God and God looks at us. We look with the eyes of our hearts and our souls. God takes the initiative and God is the achiever in all that we do and all that happens to us.

God is waiting to find us, work in us, and become an integral part of our being.

✛ 8

Reflecting on Our Prayer

Ignatius emphasizes reflection. We are to make a consciousness examination twice a day. Every week we are to go to the sacrament of Reconciliation. We are to reflect after prayer. If there is no reflection then our experience will be lost.

But what does Ignatius want us to reflect on? Ignatius wants us to focus not on what we did or achieved but what happened to us. Ignatius is interested in what God was doing in our prayer and in our everyday lives, not what we were doing. Ignatius is interested in how God was affecting us. Ignatius wants us to find God's pattern of acting in our lives. Ignatius wants us to focus on how we are achieving the goal of our lives, namely, finding our identity in the Divine and the interconnectedness of all of life. Ignatius wants us to live like Mary in the Gospels—to let go and allow life to happen to us.

Ask yourself, Is God offering me something that I don't choose to receive?

Thinking Makes It So

Ignatius insists that we master our thoughts. In the first week of the Spiritual Exercises, Ignatius wants us to bring to mind thoughts in keeping with how wonderful God is, and also keeping in mind our own sinfulness. The prodigal son, far away from his loving and compassionate father, thought about how miserable his situation was. It was this kind of thinking that made him feel nostalgic about his father's house and motivated him to return home. We too need to entertain similar thoughts that would arouse similar feelings, cause us to experience a radical transformation, and create in us a desire to return home to God our Father.

Thoughts are powerful. A good psychologist, Ignatius knew that our thoughts produce our feelings, which trigger our behavior.

Our thoughts and our perception of life govern our behavior.

✠ 10

A Way of Proceeding

Ignatius has a way of proceeding. Ignatius's focus is always on our ever-growing and ever-deepening relationship with God. For this we need to prepare and dispose ourselves so that God draws us more and more into the ocean of Divine life and love.

Disposing ourselves means becoming aware of the Divine presence waiting for us. It means offering ourselves to this Divine energy to work its wonders in us and through us. The more we empty ourselves of our thoughts, words, and deeds, the easier it is for the Divine to fill us with its presence and power that overflows into our everyday lives.

In the Ignatian method the focus is not on me, but on the Divine presence and power around and within me. Slowly but surely this way of proceeding becomes not just a set of exercises we do, but instead a way of life.

Learn the Divine pattern and allow yourself to flow with that pattern.

Clear, Critical, and Creative

In the *Spiritual Exercises*, Ignatius typically asks us to focus on just a small area of a mystery and go as deep as we can. If we follow the Ignatian pathway we excel in a field where we develop and use our God-given gifts. We don't ignore our other gifts, but our focus is on the depth rather than the breadth of our gifts and talents. We develop our strengths, knowing that this will carry us forward.

We constantly watch ourselves critically, trying to become aware of obstacles that come from within and without. In my experience, it's particularly important to be careful with selfishness—that we're attentive to not operating from our smaller self. We must strive to overcome these obstacles so that we might experience greater depth in our spiritual journey and in all of life. We strive to see things as they are, and not as we are.

I believe that we know we are on the right path on our spiritual journey when we give creative expression to what we experience. The pilgrim is often drawn beyond sacred boundaries and exposed to new horizons. Every peak is the beginning of a new adventure and growth.

Every new vista on the spiritual journey is an opportunity for our creative growth.

To Savor Is to Know

I learned from Ignatius that the food that transforms my life is the food I relish. The thoughts that make a difference are those that become an experience. The people who touch my heart are those whom I truly enjoy. The only God that I truly know is the one I have savored interiorly.

Jesus says that unless we eat his Body and drink his Blood we will have no life in us. Unless we savor God, we exist but are spiritually dead. When we do not taste God, we have a theology, not spirituality.

An experience of God is difficult to express in words, but our lives become the expression of that experience.

True knowledge is that experience where we find our identity in the Divine.

✠ 13

A Union of Hearts

Ignatius suggests that when theology becomes an experience of the heart it evokes greater reverence. It is in the heart where life decisions are made and transformation takes place. The heart is the sacred ground where we truly encounter and experience the Divine.

To me, this means that in my day-to-day interactions with people I should strive for a union of hearts more than a union of minds. With our hearts in union, Ignatius believes that even when we disagree with another, or with their understanding of life and truth, we will always listen with greater reverence and respond with greater respect.

We can always listen to the other with great reverence and respond with great respect.

Prayer of the Heart

I've experienced a great difference between meditation and contemplation as modes of prayer. Meditation uses the qualities of my intellect—namely, my memory, understanding, and will. Contemplation opens my heart to mystery and allows me to be transformed into that mystery. Meditation is the prayer of the mind; contemplation is the prayer of the heart.

In the Bible the heart refers to the core of a person. The heart is also our emotional center and the seat of tender affections, especially kindness, benevolence, and compassion. The heart encompasses both our spiritual and psychological experiences.

When we relate to people, life, and God with our hearts, we enter into an atmosphere of tremendous reverence. When we relate with our minds we experience the world dualistically; we sit in judgment of the other, and there are always winners and losers.

The heart is the source of our life energy.

✛ 15

Be Gentle in Desolation

The spiritual life never moves forward in a straight line. Growth comes in waves with ups and downs, and in a spiral movement going ever deeper. As we keep growing in our spiritual life, our downs are never as low as they were at the beginning.

When we are low, Ignatius does not want us to be discouraged and beat up on ourselves. He wants us to be gentle with ourselves; better still, we should have a sense of humor. We're to have a sense of flowing with the ups and downs of life while we maintain our inner peace and joy. To encourage ourselves while we are under a cloud, we can prepare ourselves for the sun to shine again.

Being optimistic and full of hope is an effective way to live the pilgrim life.

I am the sky. Clouds both bright and dark continually flow by.

Ignatius's Struggles

Ignatius reflected deeply and constantly on his spiritual journey. Those things that he found useful to grow in his spiritual life he put down in writing. Ignatius had bouts of desolation, agonized over scruples, was lead by false spiritual illusions, and was tempted to suicide. He learned how to recognize and overcome these temptations.

St. Paul had similar experiences. He confesses that the things that he would like to do he does not do, but the things that he hates doing are the very things that he finds himself doing. St. Paul was convinced that there were opposing spirits within him. He learned to surrender to God. When he battled his "thorn in the flesh," he realized that God's power is made perfect in weakness and was convinced that when he was weak, he was strong (2 Corinthians 12:1–10).

Just like St. Paul, Ignatius recognized the inner struggle. With the help of God, he learned how to prevail in the inner battle

✜ 17

Apparent Good

People are often tempted under the guise of apparent good when they are making progress in the spiritual life. This is certainly true for me. Good, challenging, or spectacular thoughts and desires give a passing thrill but soon leave me empty, depressed, and listless. We need a good spiritual director. We need to watch these apparent spiritual experiences more closely and deal with them effectively.

Ignatius recounts with us one of these experiences in his *Autobiography* (AB 26). When he went to bed at night he would receive so many spiritual insights and consolations that he could not fall asleep.

Ignatius realized that even though these thoughts were holy and good, they were affecting the quality of the next day in a negative way rather than in a good way. He put a stop to these bedtime thoughts.

Carefully examine exciting spiritual experiences when you are progressing well in the spiritual life.

✠ 18

The Principle and Foundation

When I first encountered the *Spiritual Exercises*, I thought that the "Principle and Foundation" was a philosophical statement. In time I learned differently. It describes a way of life. For Ignatius, praise, reverence, and service all mean the deepest possible union and familiarity with the Divine. These are not things to be done, but rather a way of being.

All created things are given to us to help us to attain our life's goal, namely, deepening our relationship with the Divine. We can use these gifts of creation to help us, or let them become an obstacle on our spiritual pathway. The goal of our lives is to choose only that which will deepen our communion with God.

Be still and know that I am God.

✠ 19

Being with God

Good students receive from their teachers. When Ignatius realized that God was his schoolmaster, he decided to surrender to God and allow God to direct his life. When he did this everything changed. He learned how to receive God's love and the tremendous mystical gifts that flowed with it. Living with God, Ignatius began to grow not only in his spiritual life, but also in his inner psychological freedom and mental peace.

This attitude of openness to receive God's gifts and God's love led Ignatius to a significant mystical experience in the little chapel at La Storta. In this chapel he saw God the Father addressing Jesus carrying the cross with these words, "I want you to take this man as your companion." And he saw Jesus turning to Ignatius and saying, "I want you to serve us."

In this very simple and subtle exchange we are given a profound insight into the Ignatian concept of service. Ignatius is now convinced that service does not entail doing great things for God, but being in an ever-deepening companionship with God. Of course the test of this companionship is the love that flows out spontaneously into the world without counting the cost, keeping a record, or expecting recognition or reward.

Being with God allows our love to flow to God and others.

20

False Dreams of the Kingdom of God

When Ignatius was in Barcelona to study the beginnings of Latin grammar, he was misguided by distracting spirits. During the time he set aside for study, he experienced and relished new spiritual insights. But this fleeting thrill boosted his own selfish ego. He could not concentrate on his studies. With great determination he decided not to give any attention to these holy thoughts that came to him during his time of study. He made a promise to his Latin master that he would give full attention to his studies. He was a knight who honored his word. Eventually the temptations left him.

He had a similar experience while studying in Paris (AB 82). He could not listen to the lectures because he was plagued by many spiritual thoughts that came to him while in class. He delighted in these new thoughts and would dream and fantasize how he would do great work in the future for the kingdom of God. Once again he promised himself that he would ignore these thoughts completely and stay focused on his studies.

Ignatius found his studies difficult because he began them when he was much older, and because his spirit was restless. He wanted to get out into the world and win it for the kingdom of God. But this time of study was also a time when he deepened his relationship with God.

Focus. Give your full attention to the task at hand. Temptations and distractions will eventually fade like the mists of morning as the sun rises.

✠ 21

Staying Fully in the Present Moment

One of the greatest lessons I have learned from Ignatius has been to live fully in the present moment. The past is gone; the future is not yet here. The only reality we have is the present. The past may influence our present, but it cannot control our present and determine our future.

Ignatius is a great pedagogue. He will not let us pass to the next stage of our growth until we have attained all we are capable of at the present stage of our development. This principle applies to learning a new skill, developing our talents, or growing in our spiritual life.

One of the mottos of a good athlete is reflected in the teaching of Ignatius: "'Tis the race not the goal!" It is important to play the game of life and give it our best; winning or losing is incidental.

The process is always more important than the final results.

Receiving the Grace

In the First Week of the Exercises we focus on God's love for us. We open ourselves as much as we can to take in this tremendous Divine love. Only when we are satisfied with being soaked in this love will we move into the Second Week. There, we allow this same love to continue to deepen through the hidden and the public life of Jesus. Strengthened by this infusion of Divine love we can now identify ourselves with the heart and spirit of Jesus who goes through his Passion and his death in the Third Week. Finally, the deeper we experience the gift of freedom in suffering, sickness, and death, the more we can now burst forth into the Fourth Week, the resurrection of our Lord. Every stage is a unit and part of the whole.

Every stage in the spiritual life is an essential preparation for the next stage.

✜ 23

Persevering

Ignatius wisely saw that the prayer called for in the Spiritual Exercises builds character. When we go to pray, Ignatius insists on three things: to persevere in the time we allot to prayer, find satisfaction that we have done that, and pray more rather than less.

Countless times I have seen that being faithful to the time I allot for prayer strengthens my sense of commitment to everything I undertake in my life. It seems that finding satisfaction in our faithfulness empties us of anything that is selfish. It purifies our motivations when we do not look for any reward; our faithfulness is our reward. We experience an inner freedom and deep satisfaction in life.

So when things seem difficult and you want to give up, that's when it's time to give a little more, to persevere.

When the going gets tough, the tough get tougher.

Accepting the Blessings

In good times, it's helpful to take in and receive the gifts that come our way so that we are prepared to deal with the difficult times. If for some reason you have not allowed yourself to accept the blessings that God has given you, then you might go back and receive those gifts: the good things that people said to us or the things that they did for us; the things that we did for others, big and small, that brought joy and happiness into their lives; the many situations and experiences that brought meaning into our own lives and those of others.

Good times are occasions to increase our capacity to receive the more, the better, and the best gifts of life.

✠ 25

Balance

Be cautious, says Ignatius. How often the great things that we dreamed about in a moment of excitement can become mere fantasies and never see the light of day. Ignatius would like us to come down to an even balance before we make a promise or a vow. In a state of euphoria we may not be able to see all of the obstacles or be objective in our decisions. Once we calm down we will better be able to see our strengths and our weaknesses in making our dreams a reality.

Ignatius wants us to be enthusiastic and animated about what we dream about. He also wants us to have balance and a realistic view of ourselves.

An Ignatian mystic has their head in the clouds but their feet firmly on the ground.

Paradoxical Intention

If we are tempted to something we know is not healthy, then Ignatius suggests that we do all in our power to work toward the opposite. In the *Spiritual Exercises*, Ignatius gives wealth and power as an example. He is not opposed to our seeking power and authority or acquiring wealth. But he wants us to clarify our motives. He wants us to make sure that it's not for our selfish aggrandizement but solely for the service, honor, and glory of the Divine Majesty. Our power and authority flow from our relationship with God and our wealth helps us to deepen this Divine relationship. Like Ignatius, we place all our hope in God alone.

This principle is operative in our emotional and psychological life. If we're behaving irrationally, we can pray insistently, work diligently, and live as if we are living a more productive life in peace and freedom.

Make believe that you are living this new life, and your pretense will slowly become your reality.

✠ 27

A Desert Experience

It seems obvious: a retreat means withdrawal from the busy world. But Ignatius says it anyway, and he lays great stress on it.

Jesus and the prophets went to the desert to deepen their spiritual experience. So should we. Ideally we should go away for a period of time to discover and experience and deepen our spiritual foundation.

I have often been surprised by what the desert has brought to me. I have experienced greater freedom to focus on deepening my relationship with God and grow into a greater awareness of my true identity.

If we can find times to occasionally isolate ourselves from the rest of the world, we grow more aware of how to receive the most and the best gifts that God always wants to give us.

The Mystery of the Trinity

I've read what many theologians have written about the Trinity as Ignatius read the great theologians of his day. But I think he learned more about the Trinity in one moment than he did from all the books of advanced theology he studied at the three universities he attended.

One day at Manresa, Ignatius "saw" the Trinity in the form of three musical keys or a musical chord. These musical keys were not three notes on a music sheet but an experience of the senses. He saw, he heard, and he was affected. He looked at the Trinity and he beheld the Trinity looking at him. This vision affected him so deeply that it evoked an outburst of tears with surging emotions.

This Trinitarian experience deepened within him till the end of his life. He would relate to the three Persons separately and to the Trinity as a whole. The experience of the Trinity overflowed into his daily life—any three things that he saw reminded him of the Trinity. The way Ignatius responded to the presence of the Trinity in his life prepared him for a deepening of his relationship with God.

Our experience of the Trinity is an experience of the heart.

Eucharist Brings Us to God

During Ignatius's time, Eucharist-centered spirituality was not the norm. While drafting the *Constitutions* for the Jesuits, he would frequently celebrate the Eucharist and present to God the point or problem he was working on. Often he reported receiving guidance or a confirmation through the gift of tears or spiritual visions after receiving Communion (AB 100–101).

Soon after his experience at Manresa, Ignatius began to foster the regular reception of Communion. This was a revolutionary idea at that time. On May 24, 1541, Ignatius wrote to his sister, Magdalene Loyola, that the frequent reception of the Eucharist would unite her soul with God. He also wrote to Francis Borgia, who would one day follow Ignatius and lead the Society of Jesus, that the Eucharist is the most secure and most direct way to the Divine Majesty.

In the Eucharist we are like the drop of water that is lost in the wine.

Days of Reverence

What Salvation Is

If I had to answer the question "What is salvation?" I would say Divine intimacy. This intimacy overflows through me to all of life. Love that flows from living in the Divine contains the meaning and end of all human existence. Ignatius believed that this kind of Divine intimacy is the love that humans were created to fulfill. This work of salvation is the work of God who labors for me in every creature, drawing the whole of creation into Divine intimacy.

Salvation can be understood as an experience of the beatific vision where we see God as God is and we see ourselves as we are. In this vision God is surrounded by the angels and archangels, the cherubim and the seraphim, the virgins and the martyrs, and all the faithful people of God. This is a hierarchical expression of salvation where God is the Great Other.

But Ignatius sees salvation as deification, where individuals with the whole of creation find their identity and destiny in the Divine Essence. In this interconnectedness of all life, whatever happens to one affects the whole.

Salvation is attained through a deepening intimacy with the Divine Essence.

Pray Always

One quality of Ignatius that stands out for me is his single-mindedness. He exemplified living in the Divine to such a degree that his very life became prayer. Prayer naturally integrated all his activities. But he didn't see prayer as an end in itself, nor was his work. They are means to deepen our union with the Divine.

So it is for us. Union with God must precede and give birth to the activity. This activity that flows from what we receive from God will in turn deepen our Divine union. This is the essence of Ignatian spirituality. If prayer interferes with the performance of our ministry, or if activity draws us away from God, then our approach is suspect. Ignatius insisted that an intimate union with God be maintained at all times and through all activities. The followers of Ignatius must therefore be nothing if not contemplative.

This growing union with the Divine that Ignatius intended was one that endured at all times and in every situation, both in prayer and in all actions. He wanted us to go beyond visible material creation, and experience creation as the dwelling place and the manifestation of the Divine.

Creation is a divine playground, a miracle for those who live in the Divine.

Entering the Mystery

Ignatian reverence is not a static, distant respect for God but one that comes from an ever-growing intimacy with God. Reverence for Ignatius is one of warm affection and surging emotion that draws a person into union and communion with God at the deepest possible level. In several places in his *Spiritual Journal*, Ignatius writes about how he felt his body temperature changing, his hair standing on end, and losing his power of speech whenever he was drawn through reverence into a deeper relationship with God.

Reverence, like service, is both the goal of our lives and the means to attain our salvation. Ignatius teaches us to pause before we begin our prayer, become aware of the presence of God, and fully enter the mystery we are contemplating with reverence (SE 75). We allow ourselves to become an integral part of the mystery just as if we were present, with all possible devotion and reverence (SE 114), until we find ourselves in the mystery we are contemplating

(SE 206). Ignatius wants this reverential involvement to transform us into the mystery we are contemplating. This is indicated by his repeated instruction *"reflectir en mi mismo,"* meaning to allow myself to be absorbed into the mystery.

We become what we contemplate.

Love for the Marginalized

Ignatius was committed to the underprivileged and victims of social inequality. While he was in his hometown of Loyola he paid someone to ring the church bells at fixed times every day to remind people to care for others. He worked against the kinds of gambling that destroyed individuals and families. He got laws passed to protect young girls and women who were being abused by priests and other men (AB 88–89).

When he first settled in Rome, Ignatius took the prostitutes under his loving care in order to give them back their self-respect and identity. He wanted his followers to be committed to helping the illiterate poor and their children who had no social standing.

Ignatius wanted this group of society's outcasts to be helped not only with basic care but also in the progress of their spiritual lives.

Reverence for the marginalized is wisdom.

✠ 34

Your Majesty Fills the Earth

Ignatius's "Principle and Foundation" states that we are created to praise God our Lord. In the culture in which Ignatius grew up, to praise an individual meant seeking to imitate, identify with, and desire a relationship with the one praised.

Psalm 8 helps us to understand the Ignatian concept of praise. "How majestic is your name in all the earth!" says the psalmist. The majesty and grandeur of God elicits spontaneous praise from humans. This praise silences "the enemy and the avenger." True praise comes from an intimate relationship that overshadows enemies. In this relationship of praise, the psalmist says that humans are given the realization that they are made little less than gods. Humans are crowned with glory and honor and are made stewards of creation.

The "Principle and Foundation" is the goal of our lives—to be drawn into a nurturing and intimate union with God.

Heirs of the Father

I think that the Parable of the Prodigal Son is actually about the older brother, who complains when the father restores the prodigal son. After he had slaved for so many years and never disobeyed any of his father's commandments, he complains that he did not receive anything from his father to celebrate life with his friends. The father's response is so poignant—everything the father has belongs to his son. But since the older son considered himself a slave in his own father's house, he did not know how to receive his father's offer.

Ignatius experiences himself as a Divine heir. If God is our Father then we are God's children. And if we are children of God, then, according to St. Paul's tremendous insight, we are also Divine heirs! As Divine heirs, we receive the gifts and graces of God not as a privilege but as a right.

Like Ignatius, we discover our true selves and our real identity as Divine heirs.

God loves us with a Father's love.

✠ 36

Mary, Doorway of
All Graces

Through his devotion to Mary, Ignatius experienced some of his deepest spiritual graces. At Manresa, while he prayed the Office of Our Lady he had a vision of the Trinity that brought him to uncontrollable tears (AB 28).

After he was ordained a priest, Ignatius spent a whole year preparing to celebrate his first Eucharist. During this time he prayed to Our Lady to grant him a place with her Son. This prayer culminated in another landmark experience for Ignatius. In a small chapel just outside of Rome, like Saints Dominic and Francis before him, Our Lady presented Ignatius to the Divine Majesty as her knight who would work for the kingdom of God (AB 96).

On February 15, 1544, Ignatius wrote in his journal that he believed Mary to be the doorway of all graces.

Mary, full of grace, place me with Ignatius and your Son.

Misguided Generosity

The well-intentioned spiritual pilgrim needs to be aware of misguided generosity. We may have the right intention, but our selfish egos can get in the way. This is very limiting and often self-defeating.

When we are very self-sacrificing, we sometimes martyr ourselves for life's causes. We pay a big price, and sooner or later feel frustrated and begin to give up on life and on ourselves. We are like the seed that fell among the rock when we are all excited about our intellectual insights but do not have roots, and so the seed dies. The seeds that fell among the thorns are like the times when we are charged with emotions to give ourselves for the kingdom of God. The seed grows for a little while and then gets choked and dies (Luke 8:4-7).

Lord, help me to have the patience to grow deep roots in my spiritual journey.

The Desert Path

Ignatius would like us to cultivate a disposition where we are animated and live life with enthusiasm. We want to bring about the kingdom of God here on earth. Rather than doing it all ourselves, we need to make ourselves available to God. Ignatius wants us to open ourselves to God and flow with the energy of life and the universe.

Just like Abraham, we are invited to let go of our land, our family, our culture, and our gods and to look for the land flowing with milk and honey. We are invited to experience God as God truly is. But this path will always take us through the desert. And in the desert we are alone, with no road maps or traditional paths. We are stripped of all the securities that we had found in our family tradition and even in our social and religious structures. We are finally invited to sacrifice our Isaacs—God's most sacred gifts. Like Mary, we let go of everything and flow ever deeper with the energy of the universe and the Divine. We need to prepare ourselves like a good field, so that when the seed falls in that field it will bear much fruit. (Luke 8:4–8)

In the desert, we experience life and ourselves in all its nakedness and transparency.

▪ 39

Shared Gifts and Graces

One of the effective ways of growing in our spiritual life is based on Ignatius's own experience. He teaches that if we do not share the grace we receive, we will lose the grace. It's the gifts and the graces that we share that are the ones that we own. These shared gifts become the source of a deeper life that we begin to live.

Ignatius had a spiritual experience while recuperating in his home at Loyola, which he could not stop talking about. This sharing filled him with much joy and consolation. It became an integral part of his spiritual life and helped him move forward on his spiritual pathway. In fact, Ignatius tells us that because he shared his experiences with others he felt great devotion every time he remembered these graces (AB 28).

He looked for spiritual persons everywhere he went so he could share his gifts and graces. When he was leaving Barcelona on his way to Jerusalem, he lamented the fact that he could not find any spiritual person for conversations.

It may be that one of the reasons that Ignatius founded the Society of Jesus was that the world would never lack people with whom they could have spiritual conversations.

We are confirmed in the graces we share, and they become the basis for bigger and greater graces.

✠ 40

Shame and Confusion

It is interesting that when Ignatius presents the First Week of the Spiritual Exercises he brings us first to the court of honor (SE 74). He wants us to focus on an ideal king who is very generous toward a knight who has let down his king. Similarly, Ignatius wants us to focus not on our sinfulness as much as on the bountiful love of God given to us as individuals. In the presence of the unlimited generosity of God we experience shame for what we have done and confusion that we are not being punished for all that we have done and not done.

Ignatius does not use the word *pardon* in the *Spiritual Exercises* when he wants us to pray over our sins and sinfulness. The focus is on God, who like the father of the prodigal son, is waiting for us to show up so that God can show off. God is not interested in what we have done, but invites us into an ever-deepening intimacy with the Divine and the Infinite. Our response and challenge is to allow ourselves to receive everything that God wants to give us. And God does want to give us everything! The miracle is that the human spirit is capable of receiving everything that God gives us.

The more courage we have in accepting and receiving this Divine love, the more we honestly and effectively confess our own sinfulness.

✛ 41

Cry of Wonder

In the presence of such a wonderful God we see that not only are we not punished for our sinfulness, but the elements that should work against us are actually on our side working to make our lives better, more fruitful and meaningful. The angels who are the swords of God's justice, instead of punishing us, protect us and pray on our behalf. The saints, too, pray and intercede for us. The sun, the moon, and the stars continue to shine to bring us warmth, light, and peace. The trees and the earth provide food and nourishment even when we are sinful (SE 60). The banquet that the prodigal son found is prepared and waiting for us too (Luke 15:11–32).

The response that Ignatius looks for in each of us is once again the courage to receive this tremendous love with deep gratitude that wells up from the core of our being—a cry of wonder with surging emotions.

This gratitude now becomes our way of life and will affect the way we live the rest of our days.

History of Sin

Ignatius works on our minds, our hearts, and our consciousness to help us arrive at the grace that will free us from our sinfulness and enable us to live the fullness of life. The sin of the angels (SE 50), according to Ignatius, was refusing to better themselves. They did not want to use their freedom to reverence and surrender to their Creator and Lord and allow themselves to be drawn into the Divine and Infinite life.

Adam and Eve (SE 51), for their one sin, suffered the rest of their lives. They were made in the image and likeness of God. They had an insight into this reality and experienced peace and total freedom. But then garments of skin were put on them and they were drowned in the pains and sufferings of human life. They lost sight of who they truly were—sons and daughters of God, and therefore Divine heirs (Galatians 4:4–7).

But for the grace of God we should be punished and made to suffer. Instead, we sit in judgment of those who may have fallen because of some weakness.

✖ 43

Psychology of Sin

Sin for Ignatius is forgetting who we are and thus losing our personal freedom. He confronts us with the insanity of our sinfulness, which causes us to break away from an ever-loving and generous God. Ignatius wants us to focus on the goodness of our relationship with the Divine and all that it means to us. This relationship helps us discover more and more that we are God's own children. Everything that God has is given to us not just as our privilege, but as a right. This realization ought to give us more and more freedom in following our bliss every day for the rest of our lives.

When we turn away from our relationship with God, we find ourselves like the prodigal son among the swine and the squalor that is their home. We forget who we are, and what is the goal and purpose of our lives, and of life itself. We live in psychological bondage.

Ignatius wants the memory of the goodness and love of God to evoke in our hearts an intense abhorrence and disgust for our sinfulness. Then we will never go back to life apart from God.

Pray to experience ever more deeply the fullness of life in our ever-growing relationship with God.

✠ 44

Eschatology of Sin

Ignatius believes that if the love of God does not work, then the fear of hell should. And so he introduces us to the consideration of the reality of hell. Through this reflection we are asked to pray for an interior sense of the pain of loss that those who are in hell suffer. Ignatius encourages us to enter the experiences of hell using all our senses. This in-depth experience should give us a greater appreciation of the tremendous love of God for us.

According to Ignatius, those who are in hell do not accept or believe in the Incarnation of our Lord, Emmanuel, God-with-us. God became one of us to help us realize that we are one with the Divine. Ignatius's hope is that we believe from the depth of our being the Good News that God loves us totally and unconditionally just as we are.

Hell is real when I cannot or do not receive God's love.

Sin and the Cross

Whenever we pray or think about our sins or our sinfulness, Ignatius wants us always to do it in the presence of the cross. He wants us to see Christ our Lord on the cross and ask ourselves how the Creator has become human. How has the Creator come from life eternal to die for my sins? (SE 53)

The cross is a symbol of what the Most Holy Trinity is all about. For Ignatius, God created the world by pouring all that is Divine into every creature. Redemption is the kenosis, or the self-emptying, of the Son. It is through the outpouring of the Holy Spirit that we are sanctified.

In the presence of the cross we are invited to live through this self-emptying process. We are invited to be rid of our self-love, self-will, and self-interest, and allow ourselves to be filled with the Divine presence and energy.

In the presence of the cross I empty myself and am filled with God's love.

✦ 46

Two Thieves

The story of the good thief (Luke 23:39–43) is a striking example of a person who, at the very moment when he is about to be condemned forever, uses the darkest part of his personality to steal paradise. In every one of us we have the two thieves standing on either side of the Source of life. Just like the good thief, we need to make our shadow work for us to claim the light. It is through the strength of our shadow that we all tap the Source of the fountain of life-giving water that is deep within us (John 4:13–14). From the story of the good thief we also learn that when we befriend our shadow it purifies and enlightens us. The other thief resisted his shadow and lost the freedom of the kingdom of God.

In the story of the Samaritan woman at Jacob's well, Jesus teaches the woman to dance with her shadow—a dance that will bring her to the Lord, who is worshipped in spirit and in truth (John 4:1–26). Mary Magdalene, the crazy lover, romances her shadow, which results in her being the first witness of the Resurrection. Peter's impulsiveness finds its resting place in being the rock of the Church. The power position that John was seeking is found by lying on the breast of Jesus at the Last Supper. The arrogant Paul exclaims, "It is no longer I who live, but it is Christ who lives in me" (Galatians 2:20).

It is through the strength of our shadow that we tap the Source of life-giving water that is deep within us.

✠ 47

Penance

For Ignatius, penance is essential for the spiritual and psychological well-being of a person. But too much penance can be as harmful to a person as no penance.

In the life of Ignatius we see that he first used penance to make reparation for his past sins. Since he was very fastidious about his physical appearance, he decided to imitate St. Humphrey—who let his hair and nails grow without cutting them, or even grooming them (AB 19). Ignatius counteracted his early life and desire for fame by dreaming about going barefoot to Jerusalem as an unknown pilgrim, eating nothing but simple vegetables, and outshining the saints in their rigorous penance. He undertook many strict bodily disciplines and fasts in imitation of the saints. He was particularly hard on his body since he had given in to the desires of the flesh and harmed people in his life (AB 7–9).

This method that Ignatius used, he would realize later, was extreme. But it produced the effect he was looking for.

Ignatius evolved into a new man with a new way of looking at himself and his relationship with God. He discovered a new attitude toward the whole of creation.

Is there a balance of healthy penance in my life?

What Is Healthy Penance?

Ignatius also used penance to please God. After Ignatius decided to give up his past life of vanity he no longer focused on making up for his past sins. Rather, he competed with the saints in pleasing and gratifying God. If Francis of Assisi did penance, Ignatius would do more. If Dominic did something great, Ignatius would find a way to outshine him. At this stage of his life Ignatius wanted to prove to himself that he would be the one that would serve and please God better than anyone else in the entire world.

But what is penance? Reflecting and learning from his own personal experience, Ignatius came to believe that we need to find a middle way in choosing our personal penance. Extreme penance, or no penance at all, is not healthy for our spiritual or our psychological growth.

Penance is a form of worship of God. For Ignatius, penance was a sacred outward expression of an inner desire or experience. So for example, when we fast, our bodily hunger for food is an expression of our hunger for God. We give up something that is material as a sign of our desire to value that which is spiritual. We go on a pilgrimage or visit shrines and churches as a way of finding our deeper and inner spiritual core. And this is true of every other penance.

One bit of caution: Like Ignatius, mere imitation of the saints without integrating it into our own spirit will lead to spiritual burnout.

✠ 49

Interior Penance

Ignatius divides penance into two categories: the interior and the exterior. We look into ourselves and find our tendencies to satisfy the desires of the senses that are self-destructive. Our eyes may turn window-shopping into unnecessary or extravagant expenses, or may feed our lustful desires. Our ears may tend to invite gossip that destroys others. Our sense of smell may crave foods that may not be healthy for us. Our taste buds may not know when something we like stops being enjoyable. Our sense of touch, a powerful means to express love and affection, may turn into selfish passion.

Ignatius would like us to channel these negative tendencies into positive and life-giving energies. He would call this interior penance.

Penance is not an end in itself, but a means to attain a spiritual and more life-giving end.

Sleep as Penance

Sleep is a very effective way of expressing our inner desires and how we want to spend our waking moments. Ignatius suggests that we look into not just the amount of sleep but also the kinds of beds that we sleep in. Once again he makes a difference between temperance and penance. If we are in the habit of sleeping too many or too few hours, we need to come to a mean.

Sleeping in a bed that is too soft and pampers the body may not always help to keep the body alive and enthusiastic about life. This also may not always help us to deal effectively with the pains of daily living. But in deciding the amount of sleep and the types of beds we sleep in, we need to make sure that our health does not suffer.

At one stage of his life Ignatius would have many spiritual thoughts when he was going to sleep. These thoughts kept him awake for a long time and affected his energy when he woke up so that he did not feel enthusiastic about all that he needed to do the next day. His penance then was to put aside the good and holy thoughts and make sure he got sufficient sleep (AB 26).

Healthy sleeping patterns express a healthy spirituality.

Physical Penance

The physical penance that Ignatius suggests in the *Spiritual Exercises* may not be acceptable today—hairshirts, cords, chains, or scourging (SE 85–86). But the principles that Ignatius gives are still very valid. Like all other penance, physical penance is not an end in itself, nor does it have to go to extremes so as to harm the body. Rather, it is an outer expression of an inner desire. Physical penance is to make sure that our lower nature does not get the better of us. Physical penance is to discipline the body so that our minds and spirits are alive in a body that is healthy and not lethargic.

Regular physical exercise would be a penance for many. Running, walking, yoga, or tai chi are some of the physical exercises that discipline the body and keep it fresh for the spiritual life. Body postures while sitting, standing, or walking are also an expression of our inner state of being.

Discipline of the body helps to discipline the mind and spirit.

✠ 52

Confession Is a Celebration

For Ignatius, confession is not a sacrament of penance but of reconciliation. Confession is always in the context of our relationship with the Divine. Ignatius experienced God while he was reading the *Lives of the Saints* and the *Life of Christ*. In this context he felt an urge to make a general confession. This is also a reflection of the Gospel, or the Good News that Jesus came to give. Jesus' message was about the unconditional love of God, and in this context we experience repentance as *metanoia*—a change of heart.

In the First Week of the Spiritual Exercises, Ignatius wants us to experience God's tremendous love for us rather than punishment for all that we have or have not done. We experience God's love with surging emotions (SE 60), and this experience leads us naturally to make a general confession of our lives.

Confession for Ignatius is a celebration and conversation about the experience of God in our lives.

General Confession

Ignatius gives us three advantages for making a general confession (SE 44). There is a moral advantage. Even if we are not obliged to make a general confession of our lives but rather choose to do it once a year, there is greater personal profit and merit. It gives us an opportunity to experience real sorrow for the negative parts of our lives.

There is also a psychological advantage. In going over the way we lived the past year, we will be able to have an intimate understanding of ourselves, with new insight into the patterns of our lives.

The third is a spiritual advantage. The general confession of our sins will help us become better disposed to receive all the graces available through this sacrament. We are also sensitive and open to all the graces that are present in our everyday lives.

According to Ignatius, there are three distinct advantages to confession: moral, psychological, and spiritual.

Days of Contemplation

How Ignatius Saw the Human Jesus

It's often said that we need to work hard at appreciating the human Jesus. In some ways, it's easier to see Jesus as God than to see Jesus as human. In that light, I think that Ignatius's mystical vision of the human Jesus is very surprising. He sees Jesus not as a man but as a Divine person, neither male nor female. In this experience Ignatius discovered the essence of a human being as the image and likeness of God.

About twenty-five years after his experience at Manresa, Ignatius wrote in his *Spiritual Journal* that in the humanity of Jesus he experienced the whole being of God. In the *Spiritual Exercises* he sees the human Jesus as the Creator on the cross who became man in order to die for my sins (SE 53). He portrays Jesus as assuming the role of the Holy Spirit (SE 224). Ignatius wants us to know, love, and follow Jesus intimately during his hidden and public life (SE 104). He wants us to identify ourselves with the heart and spirit of this Emmanuel during his Passion and death on the cross (SE 203), and finally become one with this Divine Essence who is risen and lives forever in spirit and truth (SE 221, 237).

The human Jesus is the gateway to the Most Holy Trinity and the path to the Divine Essence.

The King

The First Week of the Spiritual Exercises ends with us in the presence of the cross and asking the questions: What have I done for Christ? What am I doing for Christ? What ought I to do for Christ (SE 53)?

Ignatius wants us to be sensitive to the voice of God and follow God's wishes and desires. To help us do this he gives us the example of a human king chosen by God to bring the whole world into the kingdom of God. This human king invites people to join him and share his life—to eat with him, dress like him, to labor with him (SE 93). The more we open ourselves to receive this relationship, the more we will respond to the challenges of life without counting the cost, keeping a record, or seeking a reward.

The desire to do great things for the King—our Lord—is channeled into a deeper relationship with God.

✠ 56

To Know, to Love, and to Follow

In the king exercise, Ignatius introduces us to an intimate and covenantal relationship with God. In the rest of the Spiritual Exercises this relationship will keep growing deeper until we are lost and found in God.

While we contemplate the hidden and the public life of our Lord, we pray that we may know ever more intensely God-with-us, Emmanuel, loving more intimately and following this God into an ever-deeper love relationship.

The method of praying will now change from meditation to contemplation and become a way of life in the "Application of the Senses." The prayer experience will move from the prayer of the mind to the prayer of the heart, until it becomes a prayer of consciousness.

Ignatius converts the energy of doing into the celebration of being.

The Incarnation

When we think about the mystery of the Incarnation (SE 101) we need to ask ourselves, if Adam and Eve had not sinned would Jesus have been born? Did Jesus become human in order to make up for the disobedience of Adam and Eve and open the gates of heaven? Or did Jesus come into the world to show us how to be fully human, draw us into the consciousness of who we truly are, and help us experience the fullness of life?

The context in which Ignatius wants us to make this prayer is in the presence of the cross. The cross is not a symbol of our sinfulness but a sign of the greatest manifestation of love.

The grace that Ignatius wants us to look for in the mysteries we continue to encounter is an interior knowledge, intimate love, and a close following of Emmanuel.

We grow slowly and consciously into the Divine Essence.

✠ 58

The Encounter with Angel Gabriel

The angel Gabriel announces to Mary that she will bear Jesus, the Son of the Most High, whose kingdom will have no end. Mary is perplexed and asks how this will happen since she is not married. Angel Gabriel assures her that the Holy Spirit will come upon her and the power of the Most High will overshadow her. This is the same power of the wind that hovered over the darkness and brought forth a beautiful creation in the very beginning of the book of Genesis.

God offers Mary both a sign and a model. Her cousin Elizabeth had conceived in her old age, proving that nothing is impossible with God. The best compliment that Elizabeth paid Mary was: Blessed is she who believes. Mary believes all that God communicates to her through the angel Gabriel. And blessed are we if we believe that Mary's experience will be ours, too. I allow the assurance of the angel Gabriel to Mary to penetrate my own being as if these words were addressed to me personally.

What does it feel like to experience the power of the Most High overshadowing me?

✠ 59

Mary's Response

"Here am I, the servant of the Lord; let it be with me according to your word." (Luke 1:38). Mary's response is not a yes or a no but rather, "Let life happen to me." When good things happen in Mary's life, she accepts the good and celebrates it without clinging to it. And during the painful times in life, she flows with the pain without clinging to either the good or the painful. When life becomes incomprehensible, she ponders it in her heart knowing fully that life always offers its best gifts. No wonder in the darkest moment of her life she is standing at the foot of the cross experiencing in her heart the power and reality of the Resurrection.

In our contemplation of this mystery, we can make the heart and the spirit of Mary our very own. We too will be able to open ourselves to receive the best of God's gifts to us and, most of all, the Divine self.

Let it be done to me.

And the Angel Left Her

It is as if the angel Gabriel seduced Mary to accept God's proposal and then left her to work out the details on her own. Her whole life is filled with a mystery that she often cannot fathom. She is confronted with the message of the shepherds when Jesus is born, and again with the visit of the Magi. She has to take the child and flee to Egypt. When Jesus grows up she does not always understand his ways. In the third chapter of Mark she even thinks that her son has gone crazy. Her acceptance of the angel's message brings her to the foot of the cross.

The Ignatian principle is reflected in Mary's way of living life. Ignatius believed that we need to work as if everything depended on God, and to trust in God as if everything depended on us.

Like Mary, I need to work fully and to trust fully, and to let life happen to me.

✠ 61

The Magnificat

Mary is so filled with the presence of the Divine within her that she cannot contain herself. She bursts forth with her hymn of gratitude and glory (SE 263). This prayer not only glorifies God for who God is, but is also an outburst of gratitude for what God does through her (Luke 1:46–56).

My soul glorifies the Lord. My spirit rejoices in God, my Savior. God has looked on the nothingness of this Divine handmaid. From now on all generations will call me blessed. For God who is mighty has done great things for me, and holy is God's name.

This prayer reflects the Ignatian process at work. We empty ourselves of all that is selfish, to make room for that which is spiritual and divine. God looks at our nothingness. That is, God does not look at our bodies, or our thoughts and feelings. Nor does God seem to be interested in all the great things we do in our lives. Rather, God looks at the Divine breath that dwells within us, and our awareness of that reality, which alone is not a thing, but our very essence. There cannot be a healthier prayer than when we can truthfully say with Mary, "All generations will call me blessed; for the Mighty One has done great things for me, and holy is his name" (Luke 1:48–49).

My soul glorifies the Lord. My spirit rejoices in God, my Savior.

✠ 62

Jesus, Born in a Cave

Imagine the entrance to the cave in Bethlehem—it's quite narrow (SE 112). We have to bend in order to get inside. Then we pass through a small section until we come to the interior of the cave, where Mary and Joseph settle down to give birth to their firstborn child. The ox and the ass are in the first room. They provide some warmth that penetrates into the inner part of the cave where Mary is being helped by the maid.

In the beginning of the Bible we are introduced to the Divine breath hovering over the original darkness and emptiness. That same Divine breath now takes the form of a human in the darkness and emptiness of a cave. This Emmanuel, God-with-us, becomes human so that we may realize the Divine breath within us as the essence of our being.

The Divine breath at work in the creation of the world now takes the form of a human in the darkness and emptiness of a cave.

The Spirit Overshadows the Shepherds

The shepherds seem to be natural mystics. They spend their time with the sheep during the day, making sure they eat and keeping them safe during the night. Given the nature of their work and their lifestyle, the shepherds did not count in the eyes of the religious people of the time. Their minds are not cluttered with theories and theologies. Their lives are naturally synchronized with the flow of nature.

In the darkness of the night, these shepherds are overshadowed by the Spirit of God. It is the same Spirit that overshadowed Mary, and it offers them the same gift of receiving God in their hearts and lives.

Like the shepherds, when we empty ourselves of our theories and theologies and allow the Spirit of the Lord to overshadow us, we will also hear the angels sing: Glory to God in the highest and peace to all of an open disposition.

✠ 64

The Flight into Egypt

When the Magi do not return to Herod, the child's life is in danger. Joseph is advised in a dream to take the child and flee into Egypt. When structures of power and tradition feel threatened they often react with fury. Herod decides to kill all the male children in and around Bethlehem who are around the same age as Jesus.

How often do the sociopolitical systems of the world not care about the welfare of children? They may not kill them physically, but they will not provide the basic necessities for children to grow in a healthy environment. Children today are the fastest-growing population among the homeless, and infant mortality is on the increase in some of the richest countries of the world.

Lord, help me to protect the innocent and care for the children.

Jesus Leaves His Home

God's call is often radical. Just like Abraham, Jesus feels called to leave his home, land, culture, and his relationship with God. He leaves the comfort and security of his home to look for the plan that God has for him (SE 273). He walks out into an uncharted path of God's imagination. He is driven from within.

Mary, too, has to let her beloved son go, and she continues her inward journey with God. Her first response continues to deepen, and Mary's attitude becomes Jesus' way of life, too — "Let life happen to me."

Jesus is now at the crossroads. Living with Mary and Joseph, Jesus was embedded in the religious and social traditions of his ancestors. His relationship with God will soon change everything.

God's call is often radical.

✠ 66

Jesus' Baptism: A Foundational Experience

At his baptism in the river Jordan, Jesus experiences God's total acceptance and unconditional love. This experience will be the foundation of the person, life, and teaching of the Jesus we know. All the other graces that Jesus experiences will be a deepening of this experience or another expression of the baptism experience. The Transfiguration of Jesus is an example of this. The Resurrection is the culmination of Jesus' baptism.

Jesus will fall back on the authority of his baptism experience for the life that he will live and the things that he will teach. In times of crisis, what will give him the strength to go through the difficult, and sometimes impossible, times will be his baptism. Together with Peter, James, and John, Jesus, too, needs the validation of the Transfiguration to help go through the seemingly meaningless Passion, cross, and death. Finally, the message that Jesus preaches during his life, and the message that continues to live centuries after Jesus died, is his baptism experience.

God loves us totally and unconditionally, just as we are.

Jesus in the Desert

The baptism experience at the river Jordan is so tremendous that Jesus is driven by the Spirit into the desert. It is in the desert that Jesus will take time to absorb his foundational experience and make it a way of life. The desert is a place where there are no distractions; there are few landmarks, no traditions or structures to guide Jesus. His past experiences and learning are of little use in the desert.

Ignatius wants us to experience the desert like Jesus. Experience the void and emptiness of the desert seeping into the depth of our being, making us aware of our own inner emptiness. In this emptiness we find the very essence of life. We experience our identity in the Divine and the inter-connectedness of all of life. With Jesus we, too, hear the voice of God:

My Beloved, I am pleased with you. My favor rests on you. My delight is in you!

The Material Things of This World and the Pleasures of Life

In the desert, when Jesus is hungry he is tempted to change stone into bread and eat. Bread represents the material things of this world and the pleasures of life. One of the main human temptations is to hold on to the material things and the pleasures of life. It is here that we find our personal worth, identity, and security. Our material possessions and the pleasures in life are good. They were created by God, and God saw that they were very good.

In fact, we need the security of material things to help us pursue our spiritual goals without worrying about the basic necessities of life. Our wealth also provides our families and our loved ones with what they need to attain their own personal life goals.

It is our duty to learn how to enjoy the good things in this life. The Talmud states that at the end of our lives we will be judged by the legitimate pleasures of life that we have not enjoyed. Heaven is pleasure! But material things and the pleasures in our life cannot be the source of our happiness and the meaning of our lives.

The source of our happiness and the meaning of our lives come from our relationship with God.

Power and Authority

We tend to identify ourselves and others by the titles and achievements of this life. Jesus experiences this human temptation when he is offered power over all the kingdoms of the world. Power and authority are good because we can accomplish much when we do not have to depend on others or need anyone's permission. But the temptation to control the lives of other human beings and determine how the world can be is self-destructive. Jesus reflects this insight, years later, when he will say clearly:

What good is it if we gain the whole world and forfeit our essence?

The Manifesto of Jesus

John the Baptist had prepared the way for Jesus to take center stage. He had fulfilled the purpose of his life and was now ready to move on. While he was in prison, Jesus came in like a whirlwind proclaiming his Gospel, the Good News that God loves us totally and unconditionally—just as we are.

Mark reveals at the very beginning of his Gospel (Mark 1:14–15) the manifesto of Jesus' personal mission in this life. The time is fulfilled because the kingdom of God is close at hand. To repent now means to believe the Good News.

In a very subtle way Jesus is reversing the teaching of the whole of the Old Testament and of John the Baptist himself. Repentance now is no longer a condition to receive God's love. Rather, repentance becomes a consequence of having experienced the Good News, namely, that God loves us just as we are—totally and unconditionally.

The good news is that God loves us totally and unconditionally— just as we are.

Jesus Chooses His Apostles

Who is an apostle? In Mark's Gospel (Mark 3:13–16), Jesus goes up the mountain to be in union with the Divine. Having strengthened his awareness of God and the Divine life within him, he sends out an invitation to people to be his apostles. He chooses them to be with him and stay close to him in all he is doing. In spending time with him, Jesus will teach them by word and example that an authentic apostle is one who is able to receive love that comes from the Divine presence.

This experience will help us realize our identity as a Divine child and and therefore a Divine heir. This experience and realization will overflow to all people and will transform the world into the kingdom of God in our day and age.

Jesus did not invite the apostles to have theological conversations or catechetical arguments, but to an experience of the heart which sets our spirits on fire and our lives free.

✠ 72

Come Follow Me

When Jesus calls his first disciples, they leave everything and follow him. The fishermen abandon their boats and their nets. They are willing to sacrifice their way of life.

Once the disciples experience the power and the meaning of their relationship with Jesus, everything they valued counts as nothing. They have found the pearl of great price and the treasure hidden in the field and are ready to sell everything they have to buy that pearl and that field (Matthew 13:44–46). Paul, too, will say that everything he once counted as profit and good he now counts as mere dung for the surpassing worth of knowing Christ Jesus (Philippians 3:7–11).

Once we have experienced God's call and have known the face of the Divine, we are invited to experience infinite possibilities—launch out into the deep.

Water into Wine

Imagine Jesus eating, singing, and dancing with everyone else at the wedding feast at Cana. Jesus, Mary, and his disciples are having a good time.

When Jesus changes water into wine in John's Gospel, it is not a miracle but a sign. It is a sign of who Jesus is and what his purpose in life is all about. In John's Gospel, Jesus proclaims that he came to give life and life in all its fullness (John 10:10). Jesus is the *Logos*—that is, energy charged with power. It was the same Logos that hovered over the darkness and emptiness in the beginning and transformed it into the beautiful creation that we now have. This same Logos now breathes into the water and changes it into a celebration.

If only we learn to receive this Divine breath, our lives will be transformed into a celebration that will manifest the glory of the Divine.

✠ 74

Jesus Cleanses the Temple

Jesus' mission in life is to introduce humanity to an intimate relationship with God. He manifests this for the first
time at the wedding feast and then moves to the temple for
the Passover feast (SE 277). The Passover feast was a feast to
commemorate and celebrate God's covenantal relationship
with the people. It was also an occasion to remind us that
we are a pilgrim people. We need to keep growing and keep
moving along our relationship with the Divine.

The temple had succeeded in ritualizing the Passover
and killing its true spirit, which was all about a relationship with God. The temple also became a place of business
and injustice. God's love could be bought in the temple.
Jesus expresses his indignation at the degradation of his religious tradition by cleansing the temple (John 2:13–23). He
sees the temple and the synagogue as institutions of injustice rather than houses of God's love and compassion. Jesus
challenges the authority of the religious leaders of his times.

These leaders ask Jesus in turn for a sign that gives him the authority for doing what he does. Referring to his baptism as his authority, Jesus then responds by telling them to destroy the temple and in three days he will build it up.

The temple that Jesus would build was not the physical temple of Jerusalem but his own body, himself. He was predicting his resurrection from the dead. But he was also ushering in a new way of relating with God.

God will not be worshipped on the mountain or in the temple of Jerusalem. God is spirit, and those who truly worship God will worship in spirit and in truth. God's spirit dwells at the core of our being.

Jesus and the Women in His Life

During the time of Jesus, women were treated very unjustly by the social and religious institutions. They had little or no authority in society, and still less in religious circles. They were considered inferior to men. They were under the authority of their father before their marriage, and their husband after marriage. It was a major transgression for a man to talk to a woman who was not his wife or daughter.

At the risk of being ostracized by society and the religious people of his time, Jesus often identifies himself with women. His own disciples are shocked that Jesus talks to the Samaritan woman (John 4:27). Jesus engages in a conversation with the Canaanite woman and is reconciled with one of his cultural shadows—women (Matthew 15:22–28). He receives the love and care of women: the woman who washes his feet (Luke 7:36–50), the hospitality of Mary and Martha (Luke 10:38–42), and the women who are with him through his painful Passion and those standing at the foot of the cross (John 19:25, Matthew 27:55–56, Mark 15:40–41). Jesus accepts women in his inner circle (Luke 8:1–3). And of course the first apostles of the Resurrection are the women.

Jesus helped the women he met find life in all its fullness. Those same women helped him to reconcile the cultural shadow that existed between men and women of his time.

✠ 76

Jesus Calms the Storm

Ignatius wants us to challenge our faith in God. He offers us the contemplation where Jesus takes a boat ride with his apostles (SE 279). Soon they are caught in a great storm while Jesus is asleep in the boat. The apostles panic and wake him up in frustration and desperation. They are appalled at Jesus' apathy.

Jesus is saddened by the lack of faith within his inner circle and reprimands them. He calms the storm and hopes for a deeper faith among his apostles. But this time the apostles marvel at who Jesus is, rather than have faith in him.

Faith in the gospels and in the life and teaching of Ignatius is not a theology or a creed, but an ever-growing intimate relationship with God.

It is an invitation to know, love, follow, and deepen our relationship with the Divine and find our own identity.

The Transfiguration of Jesus

Jesus takes the inner circle among his disciples—Peter, James, and John—to a high mountain (SE 284). While they are there, Jesus is transfigured—his face shines like the sun, and his garments are shining bright. The Transfiguration is an outward manifestation of Jesus' inner reality. It is a manifestation of the spiritual and divine reality of Jesus. In this experience, Jesus is confirmed in his relationship with the Divine, and draws Peter, James, and John into this same relationship and to realize their own spiritual and divine reality.

But Peter wants to enshrine Jesus. He wants to enclose Jesus in a booth. The infinite gifts of God are not meant to be preserved and saved for a special group of people. God and the divine gifts are universally available to anyone who knows how to receive them.

God's gifts need to transfigure us and keep flowing through us to the rest of the world.

Passion and Death: The Last Supper

The first sign that Jesus gives us to believe in him is at a wedding feast. The last one he will leave us with will once again be at a meal. This is Jesus' final way of inviting us to experience intimacy with the Divine and find our identity in accepting his invitation to eat the flesh and drink the blood of the Divine.

At the wedding feast at Cana, Jesus identifies himself with the servants as he changes water into wine. At the last meal, once again he takes off his garments and girds himself with a towel and begins washing the feet of his disciples. Jesus empties himself of all power and dignity at the feet of Peter and the apostles. He begs them to receive the love of God and the infinite gifts of the Divine.

The only love that apostles will be able to share with the rest of the world is the love that they have the courage to receive.

The Challenge to Receive Love

Jesus is fully aware of the character of his apostles and their inner struggles. The attraction of the material things of this world, honor, and power are too tempting to give up. Ignatius wants us to gaze at Jesus at the feet of Peter who will deny him, and even Judas who will betray him, or as Ignatius would say, sell him (SE 289).

While Peter finds it difficult to understand what Jesus is all about, Judas knows that Jesus has the power and is capable of taking on the world to establish the kingdom of God. He believes that if he pushes Jesus against the wall he will reveal his power and his true identity. He offers Jesus to the scribes and the Pharisees and watches in anticipation. When Jesus refuses to assert his physical power, Judas cannot deal with it and commits suicide.

Like all the apostles, Judas, too, loved Jesus, but did not know how to receive the love that Jesus offered them.

✠ 80

I Have Given You as an Example

Ignatius considers the washing of the feet as an example of Jesus teaching us how to empty ourselves and receive the love that God gives us. The love that Jesus received from the Father is the love that overflows to his disciples and to us. In the same way, Jesus wants us to take in that love so that it can flow through us to the rest of the world. This is the only way to love. Any other way of loving becomes selfish manipulation and will hurt both the giver and the one to whom it is given.

The Ignatian pathway begins with the Spiritual Exercises, where we spend a long period of time receiving the love of God. Once we are soaked with this divine love, then Ignatius would send us out to share it with the rest of the world, teaching others in turn how to receive the infinite graces of God.

Through Jesus, the Father's love overflows to his disciples and to us.

From the Supper to the Garden

Ignatius tells us that Jesus went to the Garden of Gethsemane singing hymns. He is the Lord of the Dance. There was a tradition among some of the Native American tribes that, when they captured someone from another tribe, they would dress him up and make him that evening's guest of honor. They would ask him to lead them into a ritual dance, a dance that would end in the tribe killing the dancer and eating his flesh.

Jesus is that dancer inviting us to join him in this ritual dance that will kill him, but he will leave us his flesh and blood so that we can live, and live forever. The scribes and the Pharisees refused to dance with Jesus, and the disciples were too ignorant and sleepy to join in the dance.

With Jesus, the dance of death is a celebration of life.

✠ 82

The Agony in the Garden

Jesus has a sense of his imminent passion and death on the cross. He has prepared his followers as much as he can, and now he needs to prepare himself. He takes the twelve apostles into the Garden of Gethsemane to be with him. He asks them just to watch with him and pray. But Jesus soon realizes that he cannot count on his apostles. One of his inner circle will betray him, another will deny him, and the rest will all run away. Jesus can hear the "Hosannas!" explode into "Crucify him!"

In the darkness and the emptiness of that night in the garden, Jesus once again falls back on the Divine Presence that overshadows him and the Divine breath that will be his only strength. While the apostles sleep, Jesus surrenders his innermost fears to the darkness and the emptiness of the universe.

Jesus prays to the Father that even though they will break his body, his spirit will remain alive and free.

Jesus Experiences Human Pain

Jesus may not have experienced the pains and trials of raising a family or the difficulties of old age, but he certainly knew what it was to be human. Jesus was plagued with the fundamental human temptations all through his life and now, in his passion, he experiences the depth of human pain. The pain is so excruciating that he even sweats blood while he groans, "My soul is sorrowful unto death" (SE 290).

Jesus' passion and cross are the Gospel in action. Jesus promises us freedom, not from suffering, sickness, and death, but a freedom in suffering, sickness, and the face of death. Ignatius reflects this great virtue when he insists that his followers will be as edifying in sickness as in health, in death as they have been all their lives.

It is in pain that a person's real spirituality and relationship with God is manifested.

Peter Witnesses to Jesus

After Jesus is taken away by the temple guard all the apostles run away in fear. But Peter follows Jesus from a distance. He is recognized by maidservants as being with Jesus. Peter disowns his association with Jesus. He denies knowing the man and even curses the name of Jesus. Just then the cock crows, and Peter remembers Jesus telling him that before the cock crows he will deny him three times. Peter weeps bitterly. Through those tears Jesus will show him the rainbow of Jesus' love for him—the true meaning of his life and teaching.

In the darkest moment in his life, while Peter is denying Jesus, he is also bearing witness to Jesus.

Identification with Christ in His Pain

Ignatius wants us to get to know, to love, and to follow Jesus in his hidden and public life (SE 104). Like Mary, we let the mystery we are contemplating seep into us, without making reflections and resolutions. We become the mystery.

Now in his passion Ignatius wants our relationship with Jesus to go deeper as we identify with his heart and spirit. He wants us to make that heart and spirit our very own so that in our own times of pain we, too, may experience the freedom and peace that Jesus has during his passion and death on the cross.

The passion of Christ, which is the Third Week of the Spiritual Exercises, begins with the feelings of the First Week. There we felt shame and confusion (SE 193)—shame for not valuing what God continually offers us, and confusion for not being punished for it. Like the apostles, we, too, might not have understood and accepted the life and teaching of Jesus. We feel ashamed. But we are filled with confusion because our ignorance and stubbornness does not stop Jesus from giving us what we have missed again in his passion and cross.

We now let the heart and the spirit of Jesus overshadow us and transform our pain, fear, and anxiety into freedom and love.

Forgive Them for They Do Not Know

Forgiveness comes from knowledge and understanding. True knowledge is that which touches our hearts and transforms our lives. True knowledge comes from experiencing through our nakedness the essence of who we are—the image and likeness of God and the Divine breath. True knowledge helps us understand and experience the interconnectedness of all of life—whatever happens to anyone affects all.

Lack of knowledge, or ignorance, comes from clinging to the transitory nature of things in this life and seeking our identity and the source of our happiness in them: material things of this world, what people say and think about us, and the power and authority we have in this life.

Ignorance makes our religious traditions, together with the rituals and the law that come from them, ends in themselves. Ignorance turns a deaf ear to the inner voice that comes from our relationship with the Divine.

Father, forgive them, for they do not know what they are doing.

Women Standing at the Foot of the Cross

As Jesus hangs on the cross, we find the women standing at the foot of the cross—Mary the mother of Jesus; his mother's sister, Mary the wife of Clopas; and Mary Magdalene (John 19:25). While the rest of the world is steeped in ignorance and refuses to come and see, it is these women whose hearts experience the bitter pain that Jesus goes through. Holding on to his spirit, they are standing at the foot of the cross.

These are the women who receive the love and the life of Jesus. It is the women who learn how to believe with their sixth sense. What the mind and intellect can never understand, their hearts and their intuition experience.

Through the tears in their eyes they already see the rainbow of the Resurrection in their hearts.

Days of Grace

My God, Why Have You Forsaken Me?

Jesus experiences what many in the Bible experience. God seems to elude us when we are most in need of God. Often the prophets feel abandoned by God in moments of trial. While on the one hand the prophet will complain bitterly that he felt abandoned by God when people mocked his message and left him to die, almost in the same breath he will proclaim that God loved him with an everlasting love.

We also need to let go of our familiar ways of relating with God in order to deepen that relationship with God. Sometimes when we capture and encapsulate God in a theology or an elaborate liturgy, we can lose sight of the living God. We must remain ever faithful and committed to the relationship with God and look for different ways to deepen that relationship, and more meaningful ways to express our experience of God.

Abraham was invited to leave his land, his home, his culture, his country, and even his own gods. When he felt abandoned by his past, he was open to experience God and life in a new and deeper way.

When Mary finally accepted God's invitation, "Let it happen to me according to God's word," the angel left her. In this abandonment we find our true light and everlasting life deep within us.

Into Thy Hands I Commend My Spirit

It is the sixth hour. Darkness overshadows the earth, and Jesus lets himself pass from this life into the next. Death is the greatest leap of faith and trust in our relationship with God. In a way, death is the climax of our relationship with the Divine. In the darkness and emptiness of his imminent death, Jesus' faith in God is perfected and his spirit becomes one with God.

Ignatius prepared himself all through his life for his death. He embarks on his pilgrimage to Jerusalem just as he was, without the security of any material things. His hope was in God alone. The followers of his pathway developed a preparation for death devotion that they would use once a month. Ignatius suggested that they make their everyday decisions while keeping the moment of death before them.

Every day as we prepare for our death we live life more fully.

✠ 90

Mary at the Foot of the Cross

Mary receives the body of Jesus as it is taken down from the cross. In the darkness of the night, she ponders the mystery of the life of Jesus. The heart of the mother is broken and in indescribable pain, but her spirit is sure of the Resurrection. After Jesus is laid in the tomb, Mary relives significant moments in her life with Jesus.

Mary remembers the foundation of her life when she accepted the gift that came through the angel Gabriel— "Let life happen to me!" All the things she pondered in her heart now begin to make sense and find their fulfillment: the mystery of the birth of Jesus, his life and teaching, and the pain of his passion and death on the cross. Mary makes sense of all the mysteries in her life with the refrain from her heart and soul:

Let life happen to me according to God's word.

Jesus Appears to Mary,
His Mother

The Easter apparition to Mary is not in the Gospels. But this is the first contemplation that Ignatius gives us in the Fourth Week of the Spiritual Exercises. Since the Gospels tell us that Jesus appeared to many others, it is obvious that Mary is one of those to whom Jesus appeared after he rose from the dead. Ignatius appeals to people with understanding. Why would Jesus not appear to his mother before anyone else? (SE 219) Through her painful tears, Mary is able to experience the rainbow of a new life of peace and inner freedom. Her heart and spirit reflect the risen Lord.

The mystery of the Resurrection is the culmination of our faith. Her cousin Elizabeth had paid Mary the best compliment: Blessed are you who believed. In her life with Jesus, Mary deepened her relationship with God. While Mary let life happen to her, she also sang her Magnificat ever more meaningfully: "My soul magnifies the Lord, and my spirit rejoices in God my Savior. . . All generations will call me blessed; for the Mighty One has done great things for me, and holy is his name" (Luke 1:46–49).

Blessed are you who believe.

Resurrection Known by Its Effects

For Ignatius, the Resurrection is an experience that is known by its effects (SE 223). Words cannot describe the experience, but our lives speak louder than our words. How can we describe the taste of sugar? Our responses to life's challenges are totally different. We become like a caterpillar that has woven its cocoon and then bursts forth into a beautiful butterfly. In this new existence, a butterfly can now sit unaffected on the thorns of life and make the thorns look more beautiful. The butterfly sits on the roses of life and is not affected by the thorns, but enhances the beauty of the roses.

The Resurrection is the Divine presence and glory that is manifested in all of creation.

The life of the Resurrection is to identify ourselves with the sky and watch the dark and the bright clouds of our lives go by. Let life happen to me!

Jesus Appears to Mary Magdalene

Ignatius would consider Mary Magdalene to be that cater-pillar who entered into her cocoon when she encountered Jesus and was transformed into a beautiful butterfly. Mary Magdalene was one who knew how, and had the courage, to receive the tremendous Divine love that Jesus offered her.

Once she encountered Jesus and received his loving acceptance of her just as she was, her entire way of living changed. She could give up all her material possessions. Her multiple relationships only frustrated her. She channeled her love and focused her life on Jesus and his message and every-thing changed. She found her true identity within herself and the meaning of her life in her relationship with the Divine.

Through her tears of sadness and love, Mary Magdalene was able to see the Risen Lord, the rainbow of her life. She is sent to the apostles to be their first witness of the Resurrection.

Jesus Appears to
the Women

After appearing to his mother, Ignatius tells us that Jesus appears to three women—Mary Magdalene, Mary the mother of James, and Salome (SE 300). They come to the tomb of Jesus and wonder who has rolled the stone away. An angel appears to them announcing that Jesus of Nazareth has risen as he said.

Long before daybreak, in the darkness and emptiness, Jesus rose from the dead. In that darkness, reason makes little sense. Since our physical eyes cannot see, we cannot use our past prejudice. All we have is our sixth sense to help us take in the experience without any reflections and judgments.

The Resurrection is an experience, and not a theology.

✣ 95

Jesus Appears to Two Men on the Road to Emmaus

The two men on the road to Emmaus were among Jesus' disciples. Like everyone else, they must have seen Jesus and heard all that he taught. They seemed to have had their own ideas of what the Messiah should be. Even though Jesus had given them much hope, his death on the cross shattered them. They decided to return to the lives they lived before they met Jesus.

These men tried to understand Jesus according to the tradition of their scriptures and what their five senses could take in. Jesus caught up with them as they were walking. He taught them to listen with their hearts and helped their understanding go beyond their five senses.

At the end of the day, Jesus broke bread with them and their eyes were finally opened. They understood and recognized the risen Christ and what his life on earth was all about. And they felt a tremendous need to proclaim what they experienced.

According to Ignatius, listening with your heart is the best way for owning our experiences and making them the platform for bigger and greater graces.

✠ 96

Jesus Appears to Peter

After the two disciples encounter the risen Jesus on the road to Emmaus, they run in haste to tell the other apostles. They find the rest of them excited because Jesus had appeared to Peter. The Gospel narrative that connects Peter with the Resurrection is the one when he runs with John, the beloved disciple, to the place where Jesus was buried. In the darkness and the emptiness of the tomb, the beloved disciple experiences the presence and the power of the risen Christ.

We are not given any details of this encounter. We know much more about what happened to Peter on Lake Tiberius. Jesus heals Peter of his triple denial by getting Peter to make his profession of love three times. And Jesus accepts Peter's love by commissioning him to nurture the other disciples in their love of Jesus (John 21).

He who had denied Jesus three times, is forgiven, blessed, and becomes the leader of the apostles.

Jesus Appears to the Twelve Apostles

The women who experience the Resurrection witness it to the apostles. But the empirical minds of the twelve cannot accept the women and their experience. While they are in the process of discounting the authority of the women, Jesus appears in their midst (SE 304–305). The men still need physical proof that it is Jesus and so he shows them his hands and his side. Jesus offers them his inner peace that no one and nothing can take away from them. He then breathes on them so they might now live by the breath of the resurrected Christ and find their identity once again.

The Resurrection cannot be defined by a theology nor can it be captured by the senses. It is an experience of consciousness that is known by its effects.

✠ 98

Jesus Appears to Paul

Paul claims to be an apostle because of his revelation of God on the road to Damascus. Paul never knew the historical Jesus. He counts himself among the apostles because he believes that even before he was born God had set him aside for a purpose, namely, to proclaim the Gospel to the Gentiles. God sets every person aside with a specific role and purpose in life. If that person does not fulfill that role no one else can.

After his Resurrection experience, Paul will find the meaning of his life and source of his happiness in his intimacy with the risen Christ.

Paul will confidently proclaim, "It is no longer I who live, but it is Christ who lives in me" (Galatians 2:20).

Transition into Life

I come from the Divine and return into the Divine. The final exercise of the Spiritual Exercises is the "Contemplation to Attain the Love of God." It is the contemplation to attain love. This title gives us the final purpose of the Spiritual Exercises and the ultimate goal of our lives. It is significant that Ignatius uses the word *amor* and not *caridad*, even though he uses *caridad* in other parts of the Exercises. While *caridad* is the virtue of love, *amor* is the experience of love. *Amor* transforms us into itself and overflows into the rest of life. Ignatius wants us to be so embraced by and inflamed with Divine *amor* that we can love no creature on the face of the earth except in the Creator of them all (SE 316). Our *amor* for creatures in turn draws them into the Divine.

We find ourselves in union with the Divine when we live our lives the Ignatian way. This is reflected in the two preludes that Ignatius sets down before the final exercise. He states clearly that *amor* is shown more in deeds than in words. Before one rushes out to do things for others, Ignatius quickly clarifies what this doing is all about. The persons involved in this relationship are we and the Divine. The dynamic and process of the Exercises draws us steadily into the immense Divine *amor* where we find our true identity.

It is a mutual emptying of our total selves in relationship with the Divine until we meld in amor *and the two become one.*

■ 100

The Usual Preparatory Prayer

The "Contemplation to Attain the Love of God" is a transition from our spiritual retreat to everyday life. The preparatory prayer that Ignatius wanted us to make before we began any prayer is to become our way of life (SE 46). This prayer helps us focus our entire selves on the goal and purpose of our lives, namely, an ever-deepening of our union and familiarity with the Divine.

After the retreat, Ignatius wants us to make the preparatory prayer a way of life. We begin every day with our prayer and our work, asking God our Lord to help us direct all our thoughts, words, and actions purely to the praise and service of the Divine. This prayer is an expression of Ignatius' "Principle and Foundation" (SE 23) and is meant to help us deepen our union and familiarity with the Divine in all we do and all that happens to us.

Lord, help us to direct our thoughts, words, and actions purely to deepen our union with the Divine.

✠ 101

To Love and to Serve

The grace that Ignatius wants us to experience in the preparatory prayer is a celebration of life. It is a realization of the great gifts we have received from the Divine bounty and goodness. Filled with gratitude, we will respond by letting the love we have received flow into everyone we meet and all that we do (SE 233).

We become aware of the many gifts of God with gratitude, and gratitude is a memory of the heart. Gratitude is that process where we allow the gifts we have received to touch our hearts and transform our lives. Our transformed lives help us feel more and more the interconnectedness of all of life. Therefore, the gifts that have transformed us now flow out of us because we realize that they belong to everyone.

We let the gifts of God flow in us and through us back into the universe.

The Four Movements: Recall the Gifts Received

Ignatius offers us four movements in experiencing the symphony of God's love and attaining the ultimate purpose of our lives. The first movement begins with Ignatius inviting us to call to mind all the blessings of creation and redemption, and our own personal gifts that we have received.

Every personal gift also has the same dynamic of the Divine emptying itself into us, and then, through the gifts we have received, drawing us into itself. Ignatius wants us to ponder the divine creation, redemption, and our personal gifts with great affection. This exercise is not just a consideration done with the mind and beautiful thoughts, but one that is an *amor* experience of the heart.

For Ignatius, creation is the Divine pouring itself into every creature, and redemption is the Divine drawing into itself all of creation.

The Gift of the Divine Self

Ignatius wants us to ponder with great affection all that we have received from God and how much more God wants to give us, including the Divine Self (SE 231). Ignatius experienced the infinite gifts of God in his own personal life. He experienced union with Christ when he was placed with the Son. Jesus placed him in the Trinity, and in, with, and through the Trinity he experienced the deepest union with the Divine Essence.

Ignatius once boldly said to his closest companions that after reading the lives of the saints he believed that he had received more graces than any of them. Yet at the same time, Ignatius had no doubt that the gifts and the graces that he himself had received are available to anyone who knows how to receive them.

God wants to give infinite gifts and the Divine Self to anyone who knows how to receive them in order to share them with the rest of creation.

Take, Lord, and Receive

The response that Ignatius suggests throughout the movements of the symphony of God's love is the prayer: "Take, Lord, and receive all that I have and possess . . . Give me only your *amor* and your grace, for this is sufficient for me" (SE 234).

How often we have heard that when we pray "Take, Lord, my memory," we are setting ourselves up to suffer from Alzheimer's. Or that when we offer our understanding, we open ourselves up to becoming stupid, and that surrendering our will makes us nonpersons.

This is certainly not what Ignatius wanted to convey. Instead, when our offering is one of *amor*, we are seeking to offer our entire being to the Divine process of creation and redemption. We are opening ourselves to let the Divine live through our life—mind, body, heart, and spirit.

Lord, help me to see in your movements the Divine Essence pouring itself into every creature, and then drawing the whole of creation back into that Divine Essence.

✠ 105

God Dwells in Every Creature

The second movement in the symphony of God's love is to see how the Divine dwells in every creature by its "essence, power, and presence" (SE 39). The Divine presence in the elements gives them existence, gives plants life, animals feelings and sensations, and humans the ability to understand. Therefore all of life, animate and inanimate, is sacred.

This Divine essence, power, and presence in each of us gives us life, a zest for living, feelings for others, and a way of understanding existence. We are also made as God's sacred temples and in the likeness and image of the Divine (SE 235). The words of Genesis come alive in this movement: how we are made in the image and likeness of God who breathed into us his own breath and we became human. We are the Divine breath. Or consider the words of Paul when he writes that we are temples of the Holy Spirit, the dwelling of the Trinity.

When we really want to pray, it is the Spirit within us that cries with unutterable groans. It is God who hears that Spirit and responds to that prayer. With Paul we can also say that it is no longer we who live, but God who lives in us and through us.

We are the Divine breath.

✠ 106

The Divine Is in Labor

The Ignatian God is a busy God, not a God who sits in the high heavens ruling over the universe in a detached way. The Ignatian God is one who is very involved in the life of the universe in a very real and intimate way. The third step in this movement then is to consider how the Divine is in labor, pouring Divine life into every creature to give it being and sustain its essence (SE 236).

God is Emmanuel, God-with-us, who became one of us to make us one with the Divine. The Ignatian God is one who is in labor, perfecting us who are God's temple and the Divine image and likeness. In fact, Paul believes that with God, we and the whole of creation are groaning in labor pains while we wait for the realization of our true identity (Romans 8:22). Or it is what John believes, that we will be like the risen Christ when we see him as he truly is (1 John 3:1–2).

How do we experience God laboring in the world?

One with the Divine

The whole process in the "Contemplation to Attain the Love of God" culminates in the complete commingling of the creature with the Divine.

The two metaphors that Ignatius uses are the rays of the sun and the sun and the waters of the fountain and the fountain. There are no rays without the sun, and the rays have their identity only as being part of the sun. If this example is not clear, Ignatius wants us to consider the fountain. There is no fountain without water. The water finds its identity as being an essential part of the fountain. Ignatius thus concludes the whole process of the Spiritual Exercises by wanting us to realize that God and we are not one, but God and we are not two.

We have surrendered everything we have to God, and God has emptied everything that is Divine into us. We now find our true identity in the Divine Essence.

Christ Our Model

Ignatius always wants us to imitate and follow Christ in all that we do and in the choices we make (SE 344). Ignatius first went to the Holy Land just to visit the places where Jesus was—to gaze at them and touch the places where Jesus was in order to drink in the person of Jesus. When he was dragged away by the soldiers and brought back to the pilgrim camp in Jerusalem, he remembered Jesus and felt he could identify with what Jesus went through. (AB 48)

In the Spiritual Exercises, Ignatius will want us to soak in the personality of Jesus through the prayer of the "Application of the Senses." He will want us to make it our wish, desire, and our deliberate determination to imitate Christ in bearing all injuries and abuse, and any poverty—actual or spiritual (SE 98). This imitation will continue in the third level of love that Ignatius proposes, where we choose poverty with Christ, to be poor rather than wealthy, and to be regarded as a worthless fool with Christ, who was also regarded as such, rather than regarded as a wise and prudent person in this world.

Together with Ignatius, we, too, put on the mind of Christ (Galatians 3:27), his consciousness (Galatians 4:4–7), and we identify ourselves completely with Christ. We bring ourselves under the standard of Christ (SE 136–147) and make our choices in life with the heart and mind of Christ.

Faith Seeking Understanding

For Ignatius, faith is a relationship with the Divine. This loving relationship is also based on a personal experience. But our faith and our experience have to keep on growing deeper or else they will surely fade away and die. God is always bigger and greater than anything we might know about God, and deeper than any experience we might have of God. So if our faith and our relationship with God are not growing, then we might be slowly losing the gift.

Ignatius wanted his Jesuits to be proficient in their knowledge of the faith. He wanted them to be comfortable in being theologians at the Council of Trent and, at the same time, to be able to convey the basic elements of the faith to anyone in the community—old or young, rich or poor, educated or illiterate.

For Ignatius, piety had to be backed up with and grounded in theology. And theology had to be grounded in an experience of the Divine.

Daily Examination of Conscience

The examination of conscience, or the consciousness examen, has five points. The first of these begins with gratitude to God for all the benefits we have received (SE 43). We thank God every day and twice a day for the gift of creation and redemption. We thank God for emptying the Divine into the whole of creation and for the gift of redemption, where God draws the whole of creation back into the Divine.

We thank God for all the gifts that we receive, especially for the gifts of the time before our examen. Every person who comes into our lives is God's presence. Every movement within us is God moving us into a closer intimacy with the Divine.

Our daily examen is about recognizing the ways that God is trying to reach out to us.

✖ 111

Grace to Know Our Sins

The second step of the consciousness examen is to pray that we become aware of our sinfulness, which becomes an obstacle to God trying desperately to reach out to us. Our sinfulness is our inability, or unwillingness, to receive God's love, which comes through all the gifts that each day offers us. The challenge of our loving relationship with God is not what we do for God, or how we love God, but rather the ability to receive the constant and steady love that God continually pours into our hearts and lives.

At the end of the day, and at every examen, we do not stop to ask ourselves what more we could have done for God, but rather what was it that God wanted to do for us and how we did not pay attention.

We need to become aware of God's pattern of reaching out and drawing us deeper into love, and our pattern of not allowing ourselves to become one with God's pattern.

Detailed Examen

The third step of the consciousness examen is to understand God's pattern in our lives, and our pattern of responding to God's ways of drawing us into that deeper and passionate love. Ignatius advises us to go over our day before the examen, hour by hour or period by period, and become aware of our thoughts, words, deeds, and feelings.

Our thoughts are the results of our perceptions and inner beliefs. If our inner beliefs are self-defeating or destructive, we need to change our beliefs to those of the Gospel. We need to believe in the unconditional love of God and be able to see, and live life according to, this loving relationship.

Our words and our actions are influenced and affected by our thoughts and beliefs.

✠ 113

To Ask for Pardon

The fourth step of the consciousness examen is to ask God our Lord for pardon for all our faults. This is one of the two times that Ignatius uses the word *pardon* in the entire *Spiritual Exercises*. When we experience pardon for our faults we experience God's forgiveness. We only know that we have forgiven, or been forgiven, when there is nothing to forgive. We remember faults and failings of the past not with guilt, but now with gratitude.

We are grateful for our past because we see that these faults and failings have kept us close to God. They help us to appreciate the love of God all the more and encourage us to open ourselves to receive the infinite love that God wants to give us, not because we are worthy, but because of who God is.

In our weakness, God's power is made perfect.

Purpose of Amendment

The fifth and final step of the consciousness examen is to make changes in our lives, but always with the grace of God. This change will not last if we put limits on what God can do with us and through our faults and failings. If we allow God's grace to work through us, then we need to let go of our control and our way of making changes in our lives. If we change by using our willpower, we will change, but the change will be superficial. It will not only be short lasting, but may also do us harm.

We need to be open and allow ourselves to receive God's love, letting the Divine power work wonders in our lives without imposing any limitations. This change will be a lasting one. It will create an attitude that will deepen our transformation until we become totally one with the Divine and the interconnectedness of all of life.

We need a positive attitude and confidence in what God can do for us and through us.

✠ 115

Another Method of the General Examen

There are three steps in making the General Examen. The first step is to recall all the events and experiences of the day before the time of the examen. We resonate with God's action in our lives with a grateful heart.

The second step is to review God's presence and action in our day. How conscious were we of God's presence and action? How consciously did we respond to God's presence in our lives?

The third step is to preview the rest of the day to see if there are opportunities where we can anticipate God coming into our lives. How can we consciously prepare to respond and receive God's presence and power in our lives?

Finally, we anticipate and consecrate ourselves to receive all that life and God wants to give us.

Informal Examen

There are three steps in the informal, spontaneous daily examen. First, we have to be receptive. This requires that we become aware of all our experiences, both physical and spiritual. We need to pay attention to the way our bodies respond to outside stimulus at various times of the day. We stay in touch with our thoughts and our feelings about different situations. We are in touch with the movements of the good and the evil spirit acting within us.

The next step is to be reflective. We stop to think about how the experience is affecting us. If this experience takes us toward God, then we know we are in consolation and it is the good spirit that is guiding us. If the experience is taking us away from God, then we are being led into desolation and the evil spirit is active in our lives.

The third step is our response. We either deepen the direction of the good spirit with an act of gratitude, or steer the action of the evil spirit away from us by confronting it with the help of God. These three steps work in unison and slowly become our automatic response in every situation of our day. These automatic responses, then, become our authentic way of living.

We seek the God who is seeking us.

Final Blessing

I remember the story of the Jesuit who came back to his community after his retreat and complained, "I made an excellent retreat but what is the use?—because none of you have changed." After you have gone through the pages of this book and gathered the fruit of your prayer, I have no doubt that your world may not have changed but you will certainly have a new way of dealing with every person and situation in a life-giving way.

You began by dealing with the aspects of the caterpillar in you, and then had the courage to enter into the darkness of the cocoon, and finally you evolved as a beautiful butterfly. Your world may not have changed, but like the butterfly, you have the inner freedom to sit on the thorns of life and not be affected by them but make the thorns look more beautiful. In the same way you can sit on the roses of life and not be affected by them but enhance the beauty of every rose that comes into your life.

Every exercise in this book was meant to help you experience more and more your identity in the Divine and the interconnectedness of life. The image and likeness of God became clearer and the Divine breath now flows more freely in you and through you.

Through this book you have learned how to open yourself and receive God and the infinite gifts of the Divine and let them overflow into your relationships, work, and the universe. You have found your way of disposing yourself so that the Divine energy that continually wants to overshadow you will finally pervade every part of your being.

Remember that the challenge of this loving relationship is not to love but to receive love! The love that I allow myself to receive will flow out from me to others and to the rest of the world without my discriminating, counting the cost, keeping a record, or looking for a reward!

May God who started this good work in you bring it to completion!

Also available by Paul Coutinho, SJ

How Big Is Your God?

$12.95 • Paperback • 3294-7
$18.95 • Hardcover • 2481-2

Does your faith revolve around religion or relationship? This book shows us how to move past religion as we know it and how to move into a meaningful and lasting relationship with the Divine.

Just as You Are

$18.95 • Hardcover • 2721-9

Just as You Are encourages readers to stop spinning their spiritual hamster wheels trying to please God and to start living in the limitless love of God—the Divine gift available to anyone who desires it.

All books by Paul Coutinho, SJ, are now available as eBooks.
Visit www.loyolapress.com to purchase these other formats.

Continue your Ignatian spirituality journey online . . .

Learn more about prayer, spiritual direction,
retreats, and how to make good decisions at

www.ignatianspirituality.com